Home Comforts

The Art of Transforming Your Home Into Your Own Personal Paradise

By Ace McCloud
Copyright © 2017

Disclaimer

The information provided in this book is designed to provide helpful information on the subjects discussed. This book is not meant to be used, nor should it be used, to diagnose or treat any medical condition. For diagnosis or treatment of any medical problem, consult your own physician. The publisher and author are not responsible for any specific health or allergy needs that may require medical supervision and are not liable for any damages or negative consequences from any treatment, action, application or preparation, to any person reading or following the information in this book. Any references included are provided for informational purposes only. Readers should be aware that any websites or links listed in this book may change.

Table of Contents

Introduction 6
Chapter 1: A Clean Home Is A Happy Home 8
Chapter 2: Refreshing Décor 15
Chapter 3: Paradise Plants 22
Chapter 4: The Care And Feeding Of Visitors And Family . 27
Chapter 5: Self-Care 35
Chapter 6: Ahh, It Smells Like Paradise! 44
Chapter 7: Preserve Your Fabrics 53
Chapter 8: The Stuff That Makes Up Paradise 60
Chapter 9: Basic Home Maintenance 64
Chapter 10: A Pet's Paradise 67
Conclusion 70
My Other Books and Audio Books 71

Be sure to check out my website for all my Books and Audio books.

www.AcesEbooks.com

Introduction

I want to thank you and congratulate you for buying the book, "Home Comforts: The Art of Transforming Your Home Into Your Own Personal Paradise."

This book contains proven steps and strategies for making your home a paradise fit for a king or queen. You won't feel like leaving your home after learning how to make it into a delightful, refreshing oasis of peace. Your friends will return again and again and you will have your own personal piece of paradise.

Do people gravitate toward your home? Is your kitchen an oasis where people like to hang out and just talk? Beyond that, is home a place *you* look forward to seeing at the end of a long day away? No matter the current state of your home, this book can help you transform your abode into a refreshing oasis for yourself, your immediate family, and your friends.

Learn how to keep your home clean and tidy without it taking all day – and all of your energy! Discover principles of minimalism that will hold chaos at bay and turn your home into a haven of refreshing delight. Does your house feel cluttered? Is your attention distracted by pictures that cover every wall? Do knick-knacks gather dust in every corner, nook and cranny? Discover painless strategies to corral the clutter and pare down your possessions so that you surround yourself with what is truly of value.

Learn fresh ways to make your family and your guests feel welcome. I've included suggestions for foods and delicious drinks, all with ingredients easy to keep on hand and quick to prepare. I will also help you facilitate conversation so that everyone will feel valued and at ease.

Make your home a refuge from the world. Learn how to use color and light to soothe and re-energize. Do you wish your home could smell clean and fresh? Follow uncomplicated instructions to create a variety of air fresheners that clean the air, rejuvenate your spirits, and go well beyond just masking odors. Learn to incorporate plants into your home, not just for aesthetic purposes, but also to infuse your whole house with clean air.

Every house requires regular maintenance to keep it running smoothly. Learn how to properly maintain your appliances. Gain valuable tips that will prolong the life of your furniture, rugs, and drapery. You will also discover some often-overlooked ways to save money on your utility bills.

Even your pets deserve a refuge from the elements. Follow simple steps to keep your beloved pet happy, both inside and outdoors.

Most importantly, learn to create a paradise within yourself. Discover practical strategies for self-care that will increase your inner peace. You will then be able to extend your personal paradise to infect your entire home!

This book will give you everything you need to make your home the place you have always wanted to live in. Yes, your home can become a delightful and refreshing oasis for yourself, your family, and your friends.

Chapter 1: A Clean Home Is A Happy Home

In order for your home to become your own personal paradise, it must be clean and relatively tidy. While we each have our personal levels of comfort – some tolerating greater disarray and more germs than others – no one who is emotionally healthy will feel at rest in a filthy environment. There's something deeply unsettling about living in the midst of decaying garbage, filthy floors and mounds of dirty dishes. The inner pull toward the neat and clean is so strong that for centuries people have believed, "cleanliness is next to godliness".

It's an unending challenge to keep a home clean, especially if you live with other people. Kids tend to drop things as they go through the house. Even we adults don't always pick up after ourselves. We'll deal with the issue of clutter in later chapters. Here, my focus is on keeping things clean and sanitary enough to be safe.

This chapter will equip you to maintain the pristine paradise you are dreaming of, all without the use of toxic chemicals and complicated procedures. To keep your house clean, you may already have a host of cleaning products stashed under your sink (if not spilling out into other cabinets, as well). I'm going to show you a better, simpler way. With just a few key ingredients, you can maintain a house that sparkles. All the while, you will be avoiding dangerous carcinogens and other invisible toxins that would undermine the paradise you are seeking to create.

Key Ingredients

There are just a few ingredients you need to keep on hand in quantity. They are:

- Vinegar (white vinegar for most purposes, although there are plenty of uses for red cider vinegar)

- Baking soda

- Salt – Regular table salt in most cases. Use kosher or sea salt if you are scrubbing something, because of the added abrasive from the coarser texture.

- Borax – this is readily available in most grocery stores in the cleaning aisle.

- Water

See, I told you the ingredients were simple! The recipes for these cleaning treatments call for a variety of items you most likely already have in your cabinets.

General Cleaner

Ingredients:

1/2 cup vinegar

1/4 cup baking soda

1/2 gallon water

combine these items in a bowl. Keep your face out of the bowl, because this will foam up a bit. Mix it well, then add the water. Pour this into a spray bottle. You can store the excess in a glass jar if you have leftover liquid.

Glass Cleaner

Ingredients:

1/4 cup 70% Isopropyl alcohol (rubbing alcohol)

1/2 cup white vinegar

2 cups water

Newspaper or coffee filters

Directions:

- Mix all ingredients in a spray bottle
- Spray on the surface and wipe off with newsprint or coffee filter.

The vinegar cuts through dust, oils, and other grime while the alcohol causes the solution to dry quickly so it won't leave streaks. Do not use paper towels to wipe this off, as it will leave little bits of towel and streaks behind. Instead use black and white newspaper or coffee filters for a clean, smudge-free shine.

Floor Wash

Warning: Do **not** use on wood or marble flooring.

Ingredients:

4 gallons hot water

1/4 cup white vinegar

Directions:

- Mix the ingredients in a mop bucket.
- Mop the floor with this combination.

For really messy stains, like spilled jam or dried-on food, use a scrub brush to lift them off. Spills should come off easily after wetting them down.

Warning: Never use this floor wash on <u>wood</u>, because it will strip the finish right off. Also avoid using it on <u>marble</u> flooring because it will cause the marble to appear dull and lifeless.

Vinyl And Linoleum Cleaner

Ingredients:

1 gallon warm water, less 2 cups

1 cup vinegar

1/4 cup Borax

2 drops baby oil

Directions:

- Place the water in a jug or bowl.
- Add vinegar, borax and baby oil.
- Don't slop this on the floor with your mop because it can be dangerously slippery. Instead, pour the solution into a spray bottle, then spritz and mop a section at a time. If the floor feels a little slippery after it dries, just mop it again with a little warm water, using a fairly dry mop.

Wood Floor Cleaner

Ingredients:

- White vinegar
- Vegetable oil (NOT olive oil)
- Water

Directions:

Wooden floors call for special care. Too much moisture can warp a wood floor and cause real problems.

For this reason, you will want to put the cleaning solution in a spray bottle and work your way from one corner of the floor to the next, spraying and mopping one section at a time, instead of slopping liquid all over the floor. Only spray enough to moisten the floor and remove the dirt. Rinse your mop periodically in hot water, but wring it as dry as possible.

Abrasive Scouring Powder

Ingredients:

1/2 cup washing soda

1/2 cup salt (non-iodized) – I prefer kosher salt; the granules are coarser and more abrasive

5 drops any essential oil (optional)

White vinegar

Directions:

- Mix everything but the vinegar into a lidded glass jar or a glass cheese shaker. If you use a jar, make holes in the lid by pounding a nail repeatedly through it so the powder can come out when shaken.
- Place the vinegar into a spray bottle.
- Spray the surface with vinegar
- While it is still wet, sprinkle on the powder.
- Wait 5 minutes, then scrub with a brush and rinse. You will be surprised at how well this works.

Soft Scouring Paste

Ingredients:

1/4 cup Castile soap, grated.

3/4 cup baking soda

1 tablespoon tap water.

3 drops of essential oil (optional, for fragrance)

Directions:

- Grate the Castile soap into a bowl.
- Add baking soda and water, stirring to form a well-mixed paste.
- Add essential oil if you wish and stir well

- Store the paste in a jar with a tight fitting lid.

Whenever you need a non-scratching abrasive cleaner, just scoop out a little onto a wet surface and scrub away. If you don't use it quickly enough, the paste will mold, in which case you can just throw it out. I never let it go that long, however, because I use it all the time; it's my standard cleaner for a fiberglass shower surround and the accompanying metal sink.

Furniture Polish

I like to make my own furniture polish because it does not cake up as thickly as the commercial brands and I can choose any scent I want. This solution makes my furniture glisten.

Ingredients:

2 drops lemon oil

1/2 cup warm water

Directions:

- First, remove any dust with a microfiber cloth. Microfiber traps dirt, dust, and debris; it will make the wood ready to receive the polish. You don't want to trap any unwanted crud in the wood, so remove it before you proceed. Mix the ingredients in a spray bottle.
- Spray the mixture directly onto a soft cloth and rub it into your furniture; do not spray it directly onto the wood.
- The process of rubbing in the polish will leave the wood shiny.

You probably won't use all the polish up at once, but it will keep for several months.

Dusty Lamp Shades

Lampshades attract dust and if you have pets, they become a magnet for pet hair. An easy way to clean lampshades is with an adhesive lint roller. Just roll off the dust and hair.

The Best Dust Rag Ever

Use an old sock as a dust rag. Just slip it on your hand, spray on the cleaner, and dust away. The sock will pick up all the grime and you just turn it inside out and throw it in the wash when you are done.

Surprising Toilet Cleaners

Believe it or not, these two products can clean a toilet better than any gel toilet solution ever could and you can often find them in dollar stores for half price. — Drop in a couple **Alka Seltzer tablets** — the plop, plop, fizz, fizz stuff — and watch them go to town.

Denture cleaning tablets work in the same way; they can clean a toilet until it sparkles. Just drop two tablets in and let them fizz away. After a few minutes, scrub and flush.

Tile Cleaner

Bathroom tiles can become dull over time; this strategy should brighten them up. Wipe — or spray — the tile surface with some <u>white vinegar</u> and while it is still damp, pour a little <u>baking soda</u> on a damp rag and wipe those same tiles again. To remove the soda residue, wipe down or spray the tiles with water. You should be able to see yourself reflected in the clean tiles.

Fiberglass Cleaner

Make your own version of bubbles that scrub away grime. You can use this to clean fiberglass and any other surface. This solution is safe to use anywhere in your bathroom.

Ingredients:

1 cup baking soda

1 teaspoon regular blue Dawn dish detergent.

1/2 bucket warm water

1 cup vinegar.

Directions:

- Mix the baking and dish detergent to form a bubbly paste.
- Using a cellulose sponge, work the paste into the fiberglass. You don't have to work in sections, just work it into the entire area.
- Combine the water and the vinegar in a bucket.
- Use your sponge, dipped in this liquid, to wipe down the paste.
- Little dirt-fighting bubbles will quickly form.
- Once you are finished with the vinegar solution, turn on the shower and rinse everything down the drain.

Coffee Stains in Cups and Mugs

Coffee and tea stains just won't do when you are serving beverages to your guests. To extract those embarrassing stains from the porcelain, rub on some toothpaste and scrub. Rinse it out and your cups will be white again.

Sparkling Toilets

Another way to clean a toilet bowl without having to scrub much is to cut a Magic Eraser in fourths. Drop one in the toilet bowl and leave it in there overnight. In the morning, flush before using the toilet. The Magic Eraser should go down easily and it will take any accumulated dirt along with it.

Chapter 2: Refreshing Décor

For your home to exude comfort, we now turn to the use of decorations. The décor that graces your home need not be complicated or expensive. It isn't hard to present an inviting home. Come with me to explore simple tactics that will enable you to present a tidy and attractive paradise of a home to everyone who enters. It all starts before friends reach the front door.

First Impressions – The Approach

First impressions are important; no place is more critical than the approach to your house. If your guests have to run an obstacle course of tricycles, dollhouses, skates, and dead plants to reach your front door, your welcome may not be worn out, but your visitors themselves will be too worn out to stay for long.

The objective for this area is to set a refreshing tone from the moment visitors step onto your property. You want to remove all obstacles to your guests' enjoyment, quite literally. It's fairly simple. Just try to keep the kids' stuff in the back yard or on the side of the house. Keep the grass cut and any flowers and bushes well-tended. In winter, keep the walks shoveled and ice-free.

Painting the front door can also make for an inviting entryway. A colored door is welcoming; it indicates that someone with personality lives here. In some cultures, red is considered lucky. A blue or green door denotes calmness and safety, while a yellow or orange door indicates that warmth and joy are waiting inside.

Apartment dwellers usually have little control over the area from the parking lot to the front door, but you have total control as soon as your guests enter. Keep your entryway clean and tidy. In most cases you will be able to hang a welcome sign on your door and place a welcome mat outside. Just inside the door, welcome your guests with family pictures or joyful designs.

If you have the space, place a bench or other piece of furniture just inside the front door; you want to provide a place for visitors to rest purses or sit to remove overshoes, even if it's a wooden box or a small stool. Paint the entryway a warm and welcoming color or provide wall décor that is full of playful color blends.

Wall Decorations

You want your home to be cozy but not claustrophobic. The first step is to keep all public areas neat and tidy.

Keep collections to a minimum. Some people love to display things they have collected over the years. Interesting items scattered around for family and guests to view makes for an inviting home. Just remember, the more you have setting around, the more work it will take to maintain them.

Displays and knick-knacks require frequent dusting and straightening to maintain a clean and tidy appearance. It would be better to keep the massive collections in your home office, your family room, den or private bedroom. Instead, rotate into the public areas no more than three items of interest that can serve as conversation starters or focal points. Swap these out periodically so you don't get bored with them and your guests will find something new each time they visit.

The way you place your furnishings, the lighting, your wall decorations and the small items of interest you place about your home will go a long ways to make your home inviting. This will make your family feel embraced, safe, and secure and will cause visitors to want to visit repeatedly.

Furniture

It is important to have a variety of options for seating in your home. If you have four guests over, but only have enough seating for three, your home won't feel inviting to any of them. The furniture in a room and its placement should match the function of the room. The family room is often a place to watch television, play games or play with kids and their toys, so it should have seating that faces the television, a table on which to play games, and an area where toys can be stored ready for use.

If you have a separate living area where you do not watch television, you can place your furniture in conversation groups. A sofa, two comfortable chairs (or more), and a coffee table is a perfect configuration for conversation and visitors. Placing furnishings in a "U" shape is perfect for conversation. Here you would have a sofa as the bottom of the "U" and the two chairs as the sides with the coffee table paralleling the sofa. The "H" shape is another option. Here you place the sofa on one side with the two chairs right across making the two columns of the "H". A coffee table makes the crossbar.

You want your furniture groupings to feel spacious and inviting. Any rug should be large enough to accommodate all the furniture in the grouping. If the rug is large enough to encompass the entire furniture grouping, you can place all four legs of each piece on the rug. Otherwise, the furniture pieces should be grouped outside the edges of the fabric. Anything else will make the grouping look crowded and small. Furniture should fit comfortably around a rug for the area to look balanced.

Step inside a fancy hotel in your town and take a look at the conversation groupings they have set up in their lobby. Notice how people interact with these groupings. The arrangements should give you some good ideas for creating comfortable and welcoming seating arrangements in your home.

Your coffee table should be at least 15 inches from the edge of the sofa or chairs to accommodate sitting down and standing up, as well as traffic in and out of the area. End tables on either end of a sofa will allow for lamps, to give adequate lighting, and will provide a space for guests to set drinks. Your end tables should be at least a half inch lower than the arms of the seating that they flank.

Lighting

The public rooms in your house should have three types of lighting. Ambient lighting usually comes from ceiling lamps. Task lighting may consist of a floor lamp over a chair, a lamp on an end table, or a light over a kitchen countertop. Finally, decorative lighting often appears in the form of floor lamps or special lighting used to accentuate focal points or draw attention to items of interest.

You will want to layer the lighting in your rooms. It is also a great idea to place dimmers on the ambient lighting so you can turn down the brightness when you want a more intimate setting. Another option is to provide upward-facing can lights in the corners of the room; these lights stream a warm glow onto the ceiling and make the room appear more spacious.

Walls

Include artwork on the walls of your rooms. When hanging pictures, the center of an art piece should be at eye level to make for comfortable viewing and an inviting arrangement. Eye level is different for each person, so figure on the middle of the piece being 56 to 60 inches from the floor. If you hang a piece of art above a sofa, it should extend no more than two thirds of the width of the sofa and hang five to nine inches above the back of the sofa. Oversized pieces look most appropriate on large wall areas; in a smaller space they will dominate, rather than complement the rest of the room. If you opt for a grouping of pieces, space them between two and four inches apart.

Mirrors are another great way to take up space on a wall. They brighten an area by catching and bouncing light about a room. Judicious placement can make a room feel larger. Just one warning: avoid placing a mirror directly across from a window because that valuable light will only bounce directly back out.

Not every space on your wall needs to be filled in order to provide a comfortable and inviting atmosphere. Leave some empty space to draw attention to what is on the walls.

Windows

Natural light is always to be preferred. Avoid heavy draperies and excessively large blinds. Opt instead for sheer panels and blinds that can roll down during the night and up during the day. If you can hang your curtains five to seven inches above the top of the window, this will make the room feel much more airy. The ceiling will feel higher and the room will lose its claustrophobic feeling.

Focal Points

Some rooms naturally have great focal points. A focal point can be a large window or a fireplace. If you don't already have a focal point in your room, you can paint one wall a different color, place bookshelves on one wall, or hang a large piece of art. You then accessorize based upon that focal point.

Color

The color of your room can go a long way toward making it inviting and friendly. Decide for yourself whether you want to dabble in bright colors or stick with neutral or pastel shades. The color of your rooms should reflect your personality. If you are calm person, stick with cool gray, blue, or green. If you are warm and outgoing, you might prefer something in the yellow, orange or red family. If you prefer neutral shades, opt for beiges or whites but always introduce pops of bright color when you accessorize; otherwise, a room easily feels blah, boring, or antiseptic.

Avoid overly busy patterns on the walls to prevent the claustrophobic feeling of the walls closing in on you. A single accent wall is one thing; just don't wrap it around the entire room.

Accessorizing

The accessories you place in your rooms can add comfort, personality, and the lived-in feel of a true home. Soft pillows, warm blankets and cozy afghans make for a nurturing, comforting room. Setting an ottoman beside a chair encourages visitors to put up their feet and relax.

Avoid utmost perfection; if things are too perfect in a room, people will be afraid to move anything. They'll hesitate to even breathe for fear of ruining the perfect order. To break the confining chains of perfection, interrupt the steady stream of books on your bookshelves; intersperse them with solid items that serve as bookends or decorative items to grace empty spaces. Let a few magazines or books sprawl askew on a side table. Gracefully drape a shawl over the arm and part of the back of a comfy chair, ready to be snuggled into.

Accessories should bring an informal look to a room, but still be neat and tidy. Display items in groupings of three, varying the size, shape and texture, but providing a single trait in common. For example, a short fat blue candle would look good with a tall thin tapered blue candle in a candleholder and a medium-sized textured blue pillar candle. You can match the shade of blue or vary the shades.

Bring nature into the home with plants. This topic is so important that it will require its own chapter later. Placing flowers in vases or displaying a nice arrangement of potted plants on an end table soothes the occupants in the room. If you want a quick embellishment, switch out the switch plate and plug plates for something that is a little more ornate than those old almond colored plastic rectangles.

Minimalism

The minimalist has an advantage when it comes to decorating an inviting home. In minimalism, you only keep and display what aids you and what enhances your life. A minimalist does not need an overflow of possessions; the home feels airy and free. At the same time, a minimalist's home can be a comfortable and cozy sanctuary. There is absolutely no clutter and anything displayed conveys the personality of the individual who lives in the home.

The living room of a minimalist would have comfortable – but not ostentatious – chairs, probably arranged around a coffee table that serves as a focal piece. There's no clutter on the coffee table. I suggest you opt for a functional coffee table with drawers to hold the remote, coasters, and anything else that will be needed on a regular basis.

Some coffee tables are hollow inside with a lid that allows you to hide newspapers and magazines for later reading. This can also be a great place to store blankets for overnight guests or the occasional friend who feels cold. Some coffee tables are raised high enough to slide a basket underneath, providing out-of-sight storage.

The space behind your sofa is another great location for stashing especially large items you will need frequently, keeping them out of sight until called for. You don't have to put your sofa right up against the wall. Instead, use low bookcases or a tall thin bookcase turned on its side to rest invisibly behind the sofa. You can easily stash pillows, blankets, DVDs and CDs there for quick access.

If you adopt a minimalist lifestyle, everything will have its proper place. Countertops will be pristine and uncluttered, ready for use. The only visible items will be those in daily use and the things that feed your life with joy.

Feng Shui Principles

There is much to be gained by this ancient oriental method of ordering a home. Feng Shui (pronounced *feng shway*) comes to us from the Chinese. It is a method for bringing one's home into harmony with all that surrounds it. Feng Shui and minimalism go hand in hand; both remove clutter from the living area. In minimalism you hold few possessions, but those you do keep carry much personal significance. Feng Shui helps you decide where to place those possessions to draw attention to them and to bring the most positive energy into the home.

Both Feng Shui and minimalism promote balance between open space in the home and the placement of various objects. Even though Feng Shui is Asian in origin, your home does not have to be decorated with an Asian theme. It works well with any style of decor.

Feng Shui and Decluttering

One of the ideas behind Feng Shui is that the less clutter you have to block the positive energy, the more freely it can flow through your home. This positive energy can increase your energy levels, give your emotions a boost, and enhance both thinking and creativity.

To benefit from Feng Shui, it is important that the entire house be clutter-free. Do not ignore a single area, simply because it's difficult to deal with. Clutter in even one area can render Feng Shui ineffective.

Feng Shui Placement

The free influx of positive energy is influenced by the way you place your furniture and other objects. This gives you great control of your life, knowing that you can arrange even your furniture to your benefit.

The command position in any room is most important to observe. It usually resides across the room from the entry door, at a diagonal angle, so that that the person in this spot can see out the door at all times, but what is going on outside does not directly affect anyone in the room.

Basic Elements of Feng Shui

Feng Shui works under five basic elements:

- Wood – symbolized by the color green and indicating renewal
- Fire – symbolized by red and triangular shapes as well as light
- Earth – represented by yellow or brown and square shapes
- Metal – symbolized by white and round shapes
- Water – represented by blue and indicated by water features

In Feng Shui the house is considered a whole, a living being where each part impacts the energy of the whole. Therefore, the garden outside has an impact on the living room, the living room affects the bathroom, the bathroom influences energy in the bedroom, and so on. Everything is connected.

Chi is the positive energy that flows through a house. Its flow should be unimpeded. Sha is negative, destructive energy that can enter a home if the principles of Feng Shui are ignored. The best way to deal with sha is to prevent it from ever entering the home.

There are several ways to attract Chi to your home. Improve the curb appeal of your house. Get rid of clutter both outside and inside. Install positive energy-bearing objects near or in the home. Water from a fountain contains positive energy, so a fountain at the front door or inside the home will attract Chi.

Chi is enhanced through learning, so a bookshelf inside the house near the front door will also attract Chi. Wind chimes near a window or door also attract Chi. Other items that Chi is attracted to are crystals, mirrors, colors, art, statues or likenesses of Buddha, and certain plants. It's also important to display items that are meaningful and beautiful to you. This speaks to both the principles of Feng Shui and the dictates of minimalism.

Attracting Chi

A clear path makes it easier for chi to find its way into your house. Placing an attraction object near the door without it being in the way also attracts Chi. The front door is called the mouth of Chi because this is where Chi enters the home. Painting the door a bright color will attract Chi. Use green for wood, red for fire, yellow for earth, white for metal or blue for water. Plants near the door can also attract Chi.

The bedroom should be a restful place. The command position for the most important piece of furniture in this room, the bed, should be the farthest spot from the door but diagonal to it. A person lying in the bed should be able to see out the door. This encourages strength while sustaining calm. Placing the bed in this area helps you sleep better, it promotes health, and it brings serenity. Since most of us spend a third of our lives in bed, this is very important.

Keep electronics out of the bedroom. Television sets, digital clocks, and computers can emit electric current that can keep you awake. If you must have electronics in the bedroom, keep them at least two feet away from the bed.

The guidelines for the kitchen are similar to the basic principles of minimalism: keep only what you need, use, or love; fix or replace anything that is broken or does not work; display art on the walls that warms your heart and makes your eyes light up. The stove is considered the room's center of power. To increase the chi coming into your kitchen, feng shui practitioners recommend lighting all stove burners each day. They also encourage the placement of mirrors on the wall behind the stove, to reflect the positive energy from the burners throughout the room.

Feng shui for the bathroom echoes the basic principles of feng shui and minimalism for other rooms: keep all counters uncluttered, fix or replace anything that is broken, torn, or malfunctioning. Because water can carry your good energy down the drain with it, the basic recommendations are to keep the toilet lid closed as well as the door to the loo. Refreshing fragrances can enhance the presence of chi in the bathroom.

How you decorate your home can make a huge difference in how people feel when they visit. It has the same effect on you, even though you may have tuned out your awareness. To regain that sensitivity, pay attention to how your feelings are affected by the décor of the places you visit. When you go home, take the "temperature" of your rooms and note any areas that could use some work.

Chapter 3: Paradise Plants

When you think of paradise, what comes immediately to your mind? I think of palm trees and a lush tropical jungle. Others may envision a green forest or a garden dense with flowers. Most of the time, plants will be included in your own vision of paradise.

One way to create a paradise in your own home is to introduce plants and flowers. Living plants add character and texture to your interior design. Not only do plants beautify the home, they also infuse it with oxygen. We humans need oxygen to live, so surrounding yourself with sources of fresh air is highly recommended.

We also exhale carbon dioxide. Plants take in carbon dioxide, process it, and replace it with oxygen. This is perfect for humans! Plants remove the bad air we breathe out and infuse the atmosphere around them with freshly oxygenated air for us to inhale. They cleanse the air, making it more safe for us to breathe.

Plants also release humidity into the air, making your home a haven for healthy breathing in both summer air conditioning and when the heat is running during the winter. They can purge the air of many of the toxic chemicals emitted by rugs, curtains and flooring, minimizing allergic reactions and allowing your immune system to function optimally. The perfect plant population for air purification is two plants per 100 square feet of living space.

Plants are a prominent feature of Feng Shui. We've already discussed the value of attracting good energy – called "chi" – to your home. Plants, appropriately placed, attract chi.

Large rooms, especially those with high, cathedral ceilings, are ideal for plants that are tall and broad. A single tiny plant would get lost in such a massive room, although a tiered grouping of small and medium-sized plants could make a delightful statement. By the same token, small rooms look even smaller with a large potted plant dominating the space. In all rooms, potted plants look nice up against wallpaper. However, watch the type of pattern you use. Large foliage plants do well up against a simple design but might get lost before a busy pattern. Wood paneled walls, on the other hand do a good job of visually setting off plants, especially climbing vines.

Warning: some plants are toxic if consumed, so take note and keep them away from children and pets. Other plants can cause allergic reactions in some people if handled.

The following plants are recommended for use in homes:

- Aloe Vera – Aloe not only cleans the air of formaldehyde and other toxins, but breaking open a leaf and placing the juice on a burn can facilitate healing. Aloe has bright green fleshy leaves. It grows best in high light and is happiest in southward-facing windowsills.

- Bamboo/Reed Palm – The stick-like stems and feathery leaves of this plant look tropical. It is good at removing toxins like formaldehyde from the air. It also humidifies the air in the house. This plant enjoys bright indirect light filtered through translucent curtains. Bamboo is said to deter negative energy and bad spirits. It attracts chi, especially when positioned near wind chimes or water features. It is also said to attract prosperity.

You can plant bamboo outside, to the left of your front door if your climate will support it. Alternatively, opt for an odd number of lucky bamboo stalks situated in an indoor place of prominence.

- Boston Fern – The big lacy leaves of this fern look best cascading over a pot. Boston Fern is a great air purifier, reducing the presence of formaldehyde and toxic metals like mercury and arsenic in the air. It lives best in indirect light with constant moisture and humidity; With adequate light it will thrive in a bathroom.

- Chinese Evergreen – This plant doesn't really look like a pine tree. Instead, it has large green lance-shaped leaves that grow up a single stalk, in either green or variegated varieties. It releases high volumes of oxygen and reduces formaldehyde and benzenes. It does very well in shade. **Warning:** the sap is toxic to animals and humans if ingested.

- English Ivy – The three-lobed leaves of this plant are sometimes dark green with white marbling and the stems climb like crazy. English Ivy does very well in tight spaces because it can climb upward. It absorbs formaldehyde and cleans the air of cigarette smoke. It is great for asthma and allergy suffers. It will grow in any amount of light.

- Ficus or Fig Tree – The ficus has small, pointed oval leaves; the plant resembles a tree with trunk and branches. It is an excellent air purifier that prefers indirect sunlight. It can grow to be fairly large, big enough to serve as a room divider. The ficus is attractive and can be placed in an area of prominence, preferably near a window that is located across from the front door. A ficus will lose its leaves in a draft, so avoid placing it near heat registers or near doors that are frequently opened. **Warning:** The ficus can generate an allergic reaction; microscopic particles of sap in the air can trigger reactions similar to a latex allergy.

- Golden Pothos – Golden Pothos has green leaves streaked with golden yellow and can grow in a hanging basket or climb up a trellis. It grows quickly and rids the atmosphere of formaldehyde and benzenes. Place it in an entry to the garage to eliminate and absorb fumes from your car.

- Jade Plant - The jade plant is a succulent. It does not need a great deal of water but it does need a lot of sunlight. The leaves are puffy, typical of other succulents. Jade leaves are oval and resemble coins, so the plant has come to represent prosperity. In fact, it is often called a money tree. The jade plant should be placed near the entrance of the home to encourage chi. Just be careful if you live in a cold climate to protect it from winter winds.

- Lady Palm – Palms add a touch of the tropics to any home. The lady palm is a slow-growing plant with fan-like leaves worthy of paradise. It absorbs ammonia and prefers lots of filtered light.

- Peace Lily – The peace lily grows large lance-shaped green leaves and produces a white hooded flower with a large yellow erect stamen. It absorbs benzenes found in paint and furniture polishes and helps to remove the acetone emitted by home electronics.

- Philodendron – The philodendron has heart-shaped leaves that vine generously around a room, flourishing in either natural or artificial light. The philodendron is said to lend serenity to a home and make it feel welcoming and inviting. If you train it well, a philodendron will vine up a wall and over doorways. The plant likes a lot of light. It cleans the air but – **Warning** – the philodendron is poisonous to pets and humans if ingested.

- Rubber Plant – Some varieties of rubber plant are suitable for growing indoors. Rubber plants have large leathery and shiny leaves and they produce high oxygen rates while getting rid of toxins. They like filtered light.

- Snake Plant or Mother-In-Law Tongue – The snake plant grows erect spikes of rich green that pierce upward. The plant does well in low light and is a great oxygen producer, making it perfect for the bedroom, to ensure a good night's sleep.

- Spider Plant – The spider plant has delicate long and slender leaves that grow solid green or in variegated varieties. The plant shoots multiple leaves from a stalk, making the leaves look like the legs of a big spider. The plant is perfect for hanging baskets, especially when baby spider plants form on long hanging stalks from the mother plant. This plant thrives in filtered sunlight. It purifies the air of formaldehyde and benzenes.

- Umbrella Plant – This plant has leaves that shoot out from the end of the stem like the ribs of an umbrella. It reduces benzenes and looks beautiful in the home but it requires a great deal of humidity and – **Warning** – is toxic to humans and pets.

A few flowering plants don't necessarily clean and purify the air, but they add texture and color to any home. This would include African violets and orchids.

African violets have velvety low-growing leaves and small, but brilliantly colored flowers in a variety of whites, violets, purples and pinks. Some of the blooms are ruffled and some are two-toned. They grow six to eight inches tall at the very most, and must be kept out of direct sunlight. They require watering from the bottom to avoid water damage on the leaves

Orchids produce beautiful flowers that appear on long stalks and bloom for about a month. They are tropical plants that require high humidity. Orchids often grow well when placed atop containers filled with pebbles soaked in water to generate the necessary humidity. I have also seen them grown successfully when set in tall glass containers without soil but with a tiny smattering of moisture in the bottom. Orchids are parasitic plants which, in the wild, live attached to tall trees. In your house, you can grow them in a soilless environment. They like direct sunlight in the morning and moderately bright indirect light for the rest of the day.

Make your home a paradise with a few plants strategically positioned to give you the benefit of their beauty and their air-cleansing abilities. Place large plants in the corners to brighten a room. They will set nicely on a corner cupboard or hang from the ceiling, especially if the plant likes indirect sunlight. You can easily line a few pots up on a bench in front of a window. In this case, choose low-growing plants that will not impede the view. Cascading plants look beautiful on stands in front of a window or with greenery tumbling down from atop bookshelves. You can create a delightful focal point by setting a potted plant atop an old high chair or an antique stool. One way to display small pots is in a long skinny tray that runs along the middle of the dining room table. Place tall plants on either side of a fireplace or a large picture window. Large and full plants in hanging baskets can be used to divide a room. To provide added pops of color to your décor, choose colored pots, woven baskets or even teacups as containers.

Care and Feeding

The maintenance of indoor plants is not difficult. Water them when they get dry and feed them with an appropriate water-soluble fertilizer at least once every four to five weeks during the growing season, cutting back in the winter. Watch for root-bound plants. When the roots have filled a pot, this is a clear indication that a plant needs to be re-potted into something larger or – in the case of multiple-stalked plants – divided into several small containers,. A sign the plant is root-bound is when you see roots emerging above the soil or when a plant just stops growing. If you pick up the plant, you will often see roots attempting to grow out of any drainage holes that exist. Replant your overgrown plants in pots that are at least two inches larger in diameter than the one they came out of, but no more than four inches wider.

Foliage plants need to have their leaves cleaned occasionally. Use a soft cloth and dip it in some mild dish soap mixed with water. A way to create shiny leaves is to rub a tiny drop of mayonnaise on the leaves and wipe them off with a paper towel. If your plants can get their leaves wet, place the pot in the bathtub or shower and turn the shower head on with room temperature water. Rinse off the leaves and let the pots drip dry for about an hour.

Plants lend a lovely ambiance to the home, freshen the air, and make it look comfortable and feel, well, homely. They help to ensure that people feel welcome. The next chapter will give you more strategies for making your family feel loved and your guests feel part of the family, whenever they visit.

Chapter 4: The Care And Feeding Of Visitors And Family

We all want our visitors to feel at home and our family to feel safe and comfortable. We don't to scare visitors on their first visit, but to welcome them and provide an atmosphere that is both refreshing and enlivening. That is the primary role of hospitality.

Hospitality is not learned overnight. As a skilled host, you will have thought ahead of time and prepared all the little things that make guests feel comfortable. Your visitors will keep coming back because of how they were welcomed and set at ease.

Visitors need to feel comfortable and welcomed into your home. You create a welcoming atmosphere by ensuring that your house is clean when visitors come to call. Of course, you will already be following the instructions in previous chapters on a regular basis, so your house will be ready to receive guests with minimal pick-up and preparation.

Make a Good Impression

You want any visit to get off on the right foot. Making a good impression starts at your front door. In addition to providing a clutter-free entryway, you can hang a seasonal wreath on the door and ensure that the windows are sparkling clean.

Answer the door as quickly as possible so guests do not have to linger on your front porch, wondering if they're welcome (or what you're scurrying around to hide). You should always greet guests personally at the door. Don't send someone else to do the job and don't – please don't – yell at them from where you are to come in. When you greet each person at the door, this enables you to welcome your guest, see to any immediate needs (restroom, etc.), and ensure that each person is introduced to someone they will find it easy to converse with.

I have been in a situation before, where the host asked me to remove my shoes before coming into her house. She said no one wore shoes on her carpet and when I finally entered, I understood why. The plush carpet was a sea of brilliant white stretching down the hallway and on across the living room. While removing one's shoes is a common practice in other cultures, I did not expect it here, and experienced mild discomfort at her request. I found myself wondering about the socks I had put on that morning; did they have any holes? What if I hadn't cut my toenails in a while? And, heaven help the person suffering from toenail fungus! I don't want people to see my feet at a dinner party!

My suggestion is: unless you provide slippers for your visitors, don't ask your guests to remove their shoes before entering your house.

Greeting

Greet guests with a handshake, a hug, or a kiss, depending on your comfort level and how well you know them. Welcome friends of your guests with a handshake as you repeat their name. The simple act of human touch can break the ice and makes a person feel valued and welcome. Even if you can't remember the person's name later and have to ask again, that initial mention of their name on meeting them communicates a warm welcome.

Following the initial greeting at the door and dealing with their wraps, it is appropriate to offer your guests something to drink. This is your first hospitable offering that says, "my house is yours; please feel at home."

Conversation

If you have invited many guests who do not know each other, it is up to you to introduce them to each other, initiating conversation that will allow them to get acquainted. Even in a small group, it may be necessary to jump-start conversations among your guests. For this purpose, I suggest you prepare some good general topics ahead of time. Research your guests ahead of time and learn about their interests, so you can introduce topics they will enjoy talking about.

Take the initiative to introduce guests you think will enjoy each other. Give them some common ground for conversation by including some interesting information as part of the introduction. For example, I would recommend an introduction like the following: "Mary, this is Darlene. She works at a non-profit that distributes knitted chemo hats to children in the hospital. Darlene, this is Mary. She is an expert at knitting and crochet." You know at least one thing Darlene and Mary have in common and when you point it out, they have a natural focus for their conversation. Another example would be: "Mike, this is Allen. He used to play quarterback for the University of Michigan. Allen, this is Mike. He coaches high school football." This places the two guests immediately on common ground.

Food

I had an Italian friend as a child; every time I walked into her mother's house, she would greet me with the word, "Je'eet?" I thought it was Italian for something, but later I discovered it was actually a shortened version of the question, "did you eat?"

You don't always have to produce a full meal for your guests, but it's appropriate to offer food and drink of some sort. This is especially important when the weather is hot. A hot beverage is almost universally appreciated, when coming in from the cold. Even if a dinner is not in the offing you could still serve refreshment such as cookies, summer sausage or cheese on crackers, cake, or fresh fruit. That's just for starters; you will find additional serving suggestions, later on in this chapter.

Sending Guests Home

You know how kids like to go home from a birthday party with a goodie bag? Adults like that too. I always provide something for my guests to take home with them after they visit my house for a party or dinner. It can be as simple as a card containing the recipe for the delicious lasagna they ate that night. You could gift your guests with the charm with which they identified their glass all evening. If you like to make homemade caramels or other candies, you could send home a bag-full. If you aren't all that crafty, just buy a few pieces of high quality chocolates and offer them to your guests as they exit the door.

Overnight Guests

When guests stay overnight, here are some things you can do to make them feel loved and to give them a refreshing visit. With a little homework under your belt, you can make it a special night for each visitor.

Settle on sleeping arrangements well before your guests arrive. Even if you lack enough bedrooms for everybody, you can still provide comfortable sleeping arrangements for your guests. If a guest is willing to take your bed for the evening while you sleep on the sofa, you'll want to prepare fresh bedding ahead of time. Sofa beds are wonderful, but even a regular sofa can make a comfy bed for a guest. Some people actually prefer sleeping in a recliner, if you have one. An air mattress can be every bit as comfortable as a "real" bed, especially if you can get one that is elevated. Keep in mind that if your guests are elderly, they may need the extra height to facilitate getting out of bed in the morning..

Use fresh bedding on each bed, include several pillows. Make available extra blankets, and give each person a set of towels and a washcloth. Provide a box of tissues. If in season, flowers on the bedside table will provide a loving touch.

Dust all furniture beforehand. Clear at least one dresser drawer for guests to use if they wish. Provide empty hangers in the closet. Provide every amenity a person would need if they were staying in a hotel. At the same time, while you don't want a lot of clutter in the room, you want it to feel like home, so include personal photographs or other decorations on the wall, an alarm clock that is easily set, a few books, a glass for water, and anything else your guest will need.

Stock up on your guest's favorite snacks. For a longer stay, seek to find out your visitor's preferred foods as well.

Unexpected Guests

Nothing is worse the unexpected appearance of a guest when your house is messy and you have no food prepared. The best defense against last-minutes guests is to keep your house tidy all the time. When you are fortunate enough to be given a little warning, here are some emergency tips for clearing the way for unexpected visitors.

Clean only those rooms that will be in use during the visit. This would include the living room, family room, dining area, guest bathroom and most likely – the kitchen. Don't worry about private areas: individual bedrooms, private baths and the home office. Keep doors to these areas closed when visitors come to call.

If you have dirty dishes in the sink, stash them in the dishwasher. If you don't have a dishwasher, put them in the oven, but don't forget they are there when you need to use the oven next time!

Keep the dining table and countertops clean, only placing on them the things that are in constant use. Keep silk flower arrangements handy for each season and set one out on the table when guests come to call.

Quickly dust off tables and shelves in the living area and wipe down the television screen.

Do a quick scrub of the toilet and sink your guests will use. Hang fresh towels and stock up on both soap and toilet paper. Remove makeup and hair styling items from the countertops and close the shower curtain to attractively conceal the tub.

Food for last-minute guests can be a problem unless you keep your pantry and freezer stocked. However, there are a few items that are quickly and easily prepared. Good choices to keep on hand for friends who drop by are salsa and tortilla chips or chips and dip. Keep frozen cookie dough in the freezer and pop the frozen cookies in the oven to cook. While providing a tasty treat (who doesn't love cookies hot out of the oven), it will also fill your home with a delightful aroma. You can freeze cooked cinnamon rolls as well, thawing them as needed. Frozen brownies also defrost quickly as they set on a plate. I recommend you also keep a stock of beverages, whether canned, instant or quickly brewed.

Recipes

You can easily pick up frozen or refrigerated cookie dough. If refrigerated dough doesn't come cut into individual servings, you can prepare and freeze individual cookie portions yourself. Just form them into balls and put them in a freezer bag. Place the frozen cookies on parchment paper on a cookie sheet and bake for about twenty minutes, without thawing, at 350 degrees, Fahrenheit.

Frozen Chocolate Chip Cookie Dough

Ingredients:

2 cups flour

¼ teaspoon baking soda

¾ teaspoon baking powder

¼ teaspoon salt

one stick unsalted butter, softened

2 tablespoons shortening

1 egg

1 teaspoon vanilla

½ cup granulated sugar

½ cup packed brown sugar

Directions:

- Combine the first four ingredients and set aside.
- Beat together the butter, shortening, egg, and vanilla until well combined.
- Gradually add in the brown and white sugar, continuing to mix until all is light and fluffy.
- Gradually add the flour mixture until it is all incorporated.
- Cover the bowl with plastic wrap and refrigerate overnight.
- In the morning, line a baking sheet with wax paper. Roll pieces of dough into 1-1/2-inch diameter balls and place on the sheet.
- Freeze for an hour, then place the balls in a plastic freezer bag and return to freezer.
- When you need cookies, take out and bake what you need, baking at 350 degrees, Fahrenheit. The dough will last up to six months in the freezer.

Homemade Salsa

Always keep some canned, diced tomatoes around so you can make salsa anytime guests surprise you. For this recipe, you will also need a green pepper, an onion, and fresh cilantro.

Drain two 14-ounce cans of <u>diced tomatoes</u> and put them in a food processor. Dice one half of a yellow or sweet <u>onion</u> and one half of a <u>green pepper</u> and add that to the food processor. Add one teaspoon of minced <u>garlic</u>, one tablespoon of <u>lime juice</u>, ¼ teaspoon of <u>salt</u>, <u>pepper</u> to taste, and three tablespoons of fresh <u>cilantro</u>. You can also add a pinch of <u>red pepper</u> flakes if you like a little kick. Pulse three times before checking the consistency of the salsa. Continue pulsing until it becomes a chunky and delicious dip for taco chips.

Popcorn

Everyone likes popcorn. You can make just plain popcorn or spice it up a bit. Add some paprika, garlic powder, or chili powder. Place the plain popcorn in a big bowl and start shaking and tasting. If you would rather have a sweet treat sprinkle cinnamon and sugar over hot popcorn.

Quesadillas

Handheld quesadillas are the perfect snack for guests. You can put whatever you want in them, including black beans, refried beans, cooked hamburger with taco seasoning added, and salsa. The way I make mine is to spread a little salsa on one side of a flat, round tortilla. You then spread on beans, corn, cheese or other delicious ingredients and fold over the tortilla in half, so it looks like a half moon. Bake the quesadillas on a greased baking sheet for about 10 minutes or until brown on top. Serve with sour cream.

Sandwiches

<u>Finger sandwiches</u> are small versions of a regular sandwich that can be picked up easily in one hand and eaten. They are perfect snacks for the unexpected visitor because they take so little time to prepare.

Make a <u>tortilla pinwheel sandwich</u> by spreading mayonnaise or ranch dressing on a round tortilla and layering lunchmeat, cheese, and lettuce on top. Roll up and cut into pinwheels. You can secure the pinwheel with a toothpick if you like.

Another pinwheel is made by mixing softened cream cheese with a little hot sauce. Spread it on a tortilla and layer with deli roast beef and thin-sliced purple onion. Roll and slice.

Quick and Easy Sweet Treats

Instant pudding only takes a few minutes to prepare; it thickens while chilling in the refrigerator. Make a parfait using vanilla pudding and fresh sliced or frozen sliced strawberries. You can also use chocolate pudding and banana slices.

Cherries in the snow is a family favorite. To make this simple dessert tear apart a store bought angel food cake into two big rings. Put half of the cake in the bottom of a rectangular cake pan. Smear a large container of thawed non-dairy whipped topping on the cake, pressing it in with a spoon. Spread a can of cherry pie filling on top of that. Place atop it the other half of the angel food cake, more whipped topping and another can of cherry pie filling. Refrigerate for 15 minutes, cut into pieces, and your guests will love it. You can experiment with other pie fillings as well.

A trifle is a dessert that uses pudding and other sweet treats to make your mouth water. Use instant pudding to speed up the process. First, crush chocolate sandwich cookies into the bottom of a bowl. You only need a thin layer. Spoon chocolate pudding on top of the cookies, then spread whipped topping on that. Drizzle chocolate syrup over the top or cover with canned pie filling. Sprinkle another layer of chocolate cookie crumbs, some more pudding, and then finish off with a layer of whipped topping. Refrigerate for 20 minutes before spooning out into bowls for your guests.

Promote Happiness in the Family

Harmony in your family makes your home a welcome place for everyone, family and guests alike. Here are a few things you can do to promote peace and goodwill in your household:

- Have dinner together at least once a week, more often if possible. If you make dinner a regular occasion on certain nights of the week, it will become a habit and, hopefully, a tradition. A University of Michigan study reports that families that eat dinner together have greater cohesion. The children were less likely to drink or take drugs. They were less likely to commit suicide or have eating disorders. The family was more likely to be healthy because of eating healthy meals at a leisurely pace. The self-esteem of each member was much higher than those who did not dine together.

Communication is probably the greatest beneficial factor, because families talk more around the dinner table. I suggest you ban phones from the table so you can give each other your undivided attention.

- In today's society it is very hard for parents to balance between work and family, but when you have kids it is essential. Avoid bringing work home. If you must, set it aside the moment you enter the house and resist picking it up until well after dinner is over.

- If you pack a family member's lunch every morning, include a short personal note of encouragement. This is a prime opportunity to let your child – or your partner – know how much they mean to you.

- Establish basic house rules and stick to them Kids – and some adults – need to know what is expected of them. If they know there will be consequences if they don't call when they can't make it for dinner or if they stay out after a certain time at night, they are less likely to violate those rules. Place the written house rules in a place the whole family will easily see them.

- Discipline should be looked upon as a teaching opportunity. This includes all kids from the littlest to the oldest. Little ones respond well to time out, but never leave them in time out more minutes than they are years old. If, for example, you have a two-year-old, your child should only spend two minutes in time out.

When the time out begins, explain why the behavior was unacceptable. A two-year-old might not grasp the full meaning, but if you start out by explaining calmly, the message will eventually get through. While there must be discipline, make sure it matters and is understood.

- Support your family members. If a child is being bullied at school, the entire family can rally to support that child. Older siblings can keep an eye out for potential trouble while at school. Parents can sympathize with the child and partner with school authorities and other parents to bring the bullying to a halt.

Families work more smoothly if everyone helps out. If one kid is on the baseball team and another is on the swim team, the whole family can pitch be present at all competitions.

- Build family traditions. Maybe you have spaghetti night every Sunday night or you have a traditional movie night with the whole family one night a month on the same day.

- Game night is a fun way for families to communicate, have fun, and get a little competitive. Set aside some time at least once a month for a game night and break out those old board games. This is a good night to welcome a child's friends as well.

- Keep organized. Nothing is worse than forgetting to pick up a kid at school or forgetting a function you had promised to attend. It can hurt if you don't show up. Keep a calendar where everyone can see it and encourage the entire family to look at it daily. Sync smart phone calendars with the family and use alarms so you remember appointments.

- Families that belong to a church or a civic group, tend to be more harmonious. They tend to have friends within another families and both families enjoy spending time together. It can boost members' sense of well-being because there are more people they know they can depend on.

- Families that know their ancestry tend to have a better sense of control over their lives. Put photos of family members on a family wall and talk about them frequently.

A happy family leads to a welcoming home that naturally sets your guests at ease. Harmony in the home is highly attractive to outsiders. When your family members are comfortable and at peace, your home paradise will be all the more inviting to anyone who visits.

Chapter 5: Self-Care

You are the heart and soul of your home. In many ways, your home is a reflection of your personality and who you are. It makes sense then that the effectiveness of your home paradise hangs largely upon your ability to nurture your inner life and express what flows from within your physical, attitudinal, spiritual, and mental well-being.

Self care is foundational to the success of your home. This chapter can make a real difference in the quality of your home paradise. The truth of the matter is, when you are living at your best – body, mind, and soul – every life you touch can benefit from who you are. Your immediate family will thrive. Your friends will be drawn to your lightness of spirit and your guests will feel the healing warmth of your personality, whether it comes directly from you or it flows through the arrangements and provisions of your home sanctuary.

Body Work

We all know it's important to guard our physical health, to get proper nutrition and adequate physical exercise to be able to perform at our best. I've written several books on the subject. The true challenge, however, is to establish a lifestyle that encourages you to do those very things we know are truly important.

I am about to give you some very specific strategies that can make a major difference in your life. These strategies will only help you, however, if you know how to make them part of your lifestyle. The secret: habit-building. It's absolutely essential that you know how to build solid good habits.

How To Establish A Habit

The key to creating a habit that carries you, well, for as long as you need it, is repetition. Not just any random repetition will do, but repetition that is practiced deliberately, without fail, for at least 21 consecutive times. This can be facilitated by tagging your new habit on to the end of activity you already perform on a regular basis. This existing habit becomes the trigger, which will activate your new habit.

For example, let's say you want to establish a habit of making funny faces to yourself in the mirror first thing in the morning. You already wash your face as soon as you get up, so let that be your trigger. As soon as you have finished washing your face, stand before a mirror, suspend your washcloth in front of your face, prepare a funny face behind the cloth, then drop the washcloth and let 'er rip! Just don't wake up the rest of the house with your laughter.

That's the first stage: focus on one habit for the first 21 days. Then, keep that habit going while you select another habit you want to build in the next 21 days. If you keep going with this strategy, you'll have a new habit firmly established every three weeks, or four new habits every three months! Just imagine how much good you can build into your life in a year, at this rate!

As you read through the strategies for improving your nutrition, exercise, and sleep, I suggest you mark the ideas you would like to build into your life. Then choose the top four items that are most valuable to you and begin implementing the first one. Before you know it, three months will have elapsed and you will have added to your healthy lifestyle with four beneficial habits!

Fuel Your Body

Here are some habits that may sound basic, but when they become a part of your lifestyle, they can have a major positive impact on your health, your energy and your alertness.

- Break free from your physical dependence on refined sugar. This is the most difficult habit of all (except, perhaps for quitting smoking). Yet, it can set you up for success in so many other areas of your life!

- At the same time, avoid entirely – or at least minimize – your use of artificial sweeteners. Their problem is in their name: "artificial." Artificial means you will be ingesting all sorts of chemicals your body wasn't designed to handle.

- Eat more fresh fruits. Instead of sugary snacks, enjoy fresh fruits. They contain so many more nutrients your body needs and they come in a world of different flavors, textures and colors.

- If you really *must* have something sweet in your morning tea, try a little honey (just a little – it naturally comes highly concentrated) or stevia – a plant-based product that tastes sweet but has almost no calories.

- Take multi-vitamins and minerals, based on your body's needs. You can often find amazing results in terms of increased energy and alertness, simply by giving your body a boost in nutrition.

- Drink water! The best thing you can do for yourself in the morning is to give yourself a big drink of water as soon as you wake up. After eight hours of no food or water, your body is mildly dehydrated. Water will take care of that problem while it wakes up your digestive system.

- Lemon water – to boost your metabolism in the morning, drink one to two cups of hot water with the juice of one-half lemon squeezed in. I can actually feel my body ramping up and burning energy for about 30 minutes after I drink this. If you can delay eating for three hours afterward, you may be able to shed a few pounds this way as well.

- Shy away from pre-processed foods. Yes, it may take a few more minutes to make things yourself, but you'll know for certain what is going into your body and you'll avoid a host of toxic chemicals that are commonplace in pre-packed meals. The flip-side of this is:

- Eat more fresh vegetables. If you don't like raw veggies, steam them! I suppose you can boil or stir-fry them, too if those are the only ways you can get them down. If you can't handle them fresh, try frozen; if you gag at frozen, try canned veggies if you must. Douse them in melted cheese, sour cream, salad dressing, or ketchup. (Although, have you read all the junk they put in ketchup?) Just do whatever you must to start eating more fresh vegetables. Later, you can do portion control on the toppings to increase the health factor and start exploring the delicious flavors of those fresh veggies all by themselves.

Move It!

Our bodies were designed to be on the move. Every part of our physical bodies work best when it is active. Muscles, joints, our digestive system, just to name a few, all are "happier" when we are engaged in at least moderate activity every day. Our activity level also affects our mental alertness and our moods. Moderate exertion releases those "feel good" endorphins.

When you couple physical activity with the great outdoors, even more good things happen. The fresh air cleanses your lungs as you breathe deeply and your whole body benefits. The additional sun exposure boosts your vitamin D content, helps regulate your sleep/wake cycle, and provides a host of other benefits.

Here are some habits you can build into your life to ensure that you are getting all the benefits of a physically active lifestyle. These are only a sample to get you started; I'm sure you can think of other ways that may work better for you. If so, use them. It's not important *how* you move; the important thing is that you get moving, and keep moving.

- Learn to fidget. If you are required to sit for long periods of time, just refuse to sit still! Swing your legs. Stretch your arms. Tense and release each group of muscles in your body. Lean from side to side. Turn your head from side to side (you can even do this while you are looking at your computer screen; just swivel your body, while keeping your eyes on the screen). Position at a distance several items you use on a periodic basis. This will force you to stand up and walk to get them. Yes, it is the opposite of efficiency theory, but consider it an investment in your physical health.

- Park farther from the door. This has the dual benefits of getting you outside and increasing the distance you walk. If you are brave enough to leave your car in a different part of the parking lot each day, it will also introduce variety into your life by giving you a different angle on your approach and will keep your mind sharp as you remember each day where you parked.

- Take the stairs. Okay, if you work on the 16th floor, don't kill yourself by walking all the way up on the first day; get off on the 14th floor for starters and take the stairs up the last two stories. After you've done that for a while, start getting off the elevator on the 13th floor, instead. As time goes on, start getting off the 'vator earlier and earlier. Eventually, you'll be able to walk the whole way; what a feat!

Take the stairs in any building you enter. It's great exercise for your legs and your heart. Even if you don't walk the entire way, every floor you climb is a boost to your heart health and your leg strength.

- Get a dog. A dog simply must be walked every day. Even if you won't walk for yourself, you may be willing to get out there for your dog.

- Join a group. If you like to run, walk, cycle, or swim, find a group you can exercise with once a week or so. This can support your own individual exercising, and provide variety to your routine. If you really want variety, pick a sport that is completely different from your usual activities.

- Use strength training to balance out your fitness. A strength training routine can provide a break from other forms of exercise, all the while working parts of your body that may be neglected otherwise. At the same time, it strengthens the muscles you need in order to better enjoy your other activities.

- Stretch. Stretching often is overlooked when we think of exercise, but it can make the all difference between stiff motion and injury-free activities. At the very least, I recommend establishing a basic stretching routine you use at the start of your day. It will work out the kinks from your muscles and gently coax your body into action, while sustaining flexibility and warming up muscles for the rigors they will face.

- Dance! Dancing is a wonderful way to burn energy, keep limber, relieve stress, and just have fun. You can dance in a formal setting, but I'm thinking more of you including dance in other parts of your life. If your comfort zone does not include dancing in the street, you can still cut a rug at home. The image that stays with me is Robin Williams' tango with the vacuum sweeper in *Mrs. Doubtfire*. You can have all sorts of fun indoors; just start the music and move. Even housework can become enjoyable when performed to music. Almost any type of home cleaning chores can be turned into fun dance moves.

Recharge Your Batteries

None of us can be all on, all of the time. In times of crisis our bodies are willing to be pushed to the brink of total exhaustion, but we were not designed to function constantly without times of rest. This is part of the rhythms of life.

Even our day is divided between rest time and time for activity, hours for sleep and hours for work, whether we're talking physical or mental activity. We need times to be "on" and we need times to be "off." Our minds and bodies benefit from downtime that allows them to process the events of the day – whether a good cheeseburger or a heated discussion. We violate these essential rhythms at our own peril.

Here are some ways you can build habits of downtime into your life:

- Go to bed. Set a specific time to go to bed at night. If you know when you need to be up and ready to face life in the morning, back that up by the amount of time it takes you to get ready in the morning. Then, back up another eight hours and that will be when you need to hit the hay the night before. Keep this bedtime consistently for a month and your body will be used to going to bed at that time, seven days a week.

- Schedule downtime. If you know you are entering an especially stressful time, Plan a day after it is all over to just laze around and do nothing! Rest, nap, read, go for a leisurely walk; purposefully choose a day devoid of stress and expectations (not even your own).

I used to do this myself. I ordered myself to stay in bed on Saturday mornings until about 11am. I used the time to pay my bills online, review and plan, think, write in my journal, pray, read and brainstorm. I did this because I knew the minute I got out of bed I would be off and running. That's just the way I was wired. It worked well for that time in my life; it kept me slightly balanced and prevented me from burning out due to over-activity.

- Make your bedroom a haven for rest and relaxation. Create your own sleep sanctuary by removing clutter from your room. Minimize the use of electronics in your bedroom and *never* work in bed.

Declare your bedroom a work-free zone. Keep the lights low, use soothing aromas, and only allow restful, relaxing sounds to enter. Over time, your body will get the message that when you enter this room you'll be relaxing and it will cooperate with you.

- Putter – By this, I mean discover the art of playing at something. Putter around, not to excel, not even to get better at it, but simply for the sake of being here, doing this. It doesn't have to be done particularly well; it doesn't even have to be finished. The purpose is to let yourself settle into just being.

We in the Western world tend to think too much. Our minds are tuned to such a fine pitch that it's a wonder we don't frazzle and break. Puttering is a way to let that tension ease off. Choose something to do with your hands, whittling, gluing montages, digging in the dirt, coloring with the kids; better yet, get your own coloring book and color outside the lines just for fun! There are a thousand things you can do to give your brain a break and give yourself some space to just *be*.

- Take a technology break. For an entire weekend, shut down the computer, turn off the phone, close the tablet, switch off the radio (even in your car), and do without television. Rediscover the true rest that is waiting for you in the place beyond the chatter. Get outside and enjoy nature. Talk with friends in real time, face to face, without distractions. Let your mind settle down in the silence. Ignore the clock and take a real rest.

Appearances Feed Reality

Our social-media focus has in some ways muddied the waters of reality, to the point that we now assume everything must be air-brushed perfect to be worthy of our attention. Then reality bites when we face ourselves, bleary-eyed, in the mirror each morning!

The challenge is to remain fully real and fully human while projecting one's self onto social media in a way that connects genuinely with other people. While this topic is too large to cover extensively here, I can at least get you started on habits that will help you express yourself effectively in the eyes of other people, regardless of the medium you use to connect with them.

- Wash your face, brush your teeth, and comb your hair. This reminds yourself that you are a valuable person; you are worthy of others' attention. You are your own best representative, so let it look like you respect yourself.

- Dress like you mean it. It's one thing to work from home in your comfy pajamas. However, as most people who work from home will tell you, how you dress affects how you feel about yourself and this is communicated clearly in your voice quality and your energy level. Dress deliberately.

- Choose to love yourself. Be kind to yourself, forgive yourself, celebrate when you've done something well. People respond instinctively to how you feel about yourself. When you are able to respond to the m from within a place of deep self-acceptance, they feel deeply loved and accepted as well.

- Dress to boost your mood. How you dress sends subtle messages to your psyche about your self-worth and your ability to handle whatever life throws your way. You can actually turn your mood around by choosing to dress a notch nicer than usual. Wear that shirt, the one that makes you feel powerful. Spend just a few extra minutes on your makeup or accessories.

When you feel good about yourself, it rubs off on other people and they start feeling better about themselves as well.

- Take a positive stance – greet friends head-on, but swiftly angle your body open slightly. This will help the person relax and enter into conversation. It will also make room for others, welcoming them to join the group in conversation.

- Take a positive stance – Let your face be straight forward toward your friends. Don't look up at them from beneath bushy eyebrows. Don't look down your nose at them, either. Both of these stances communicate judgment, not acceptance. Instead, let your eyes meet theirs in an open straight gaze. This communicates openness

- Take a positive stance – Stand tall. Imagine that your body is suspended from a string that is pulling straight up through your spine and out the top of your head, pulling your head toward the ceiling. (Don't slouch, curving your body downward.) As you practice this, you will feel more open, more confident, more self-accepting. It will enable you to interact with others more openly and freely and others will be blessed by your peaceful presence.

- Take a positive stance – When seated, let that string pull your torso and the top of your head up toward the ceiling. While it takes practice to sustain, over time this habit will serve others by bringing peace into their lives as with calm confidence you are able to care for each other.

- Listen actively – Your friends and guests want to know you actually care about what they are saying, so give them cues to let them know you are actually paying attention while they talk. Make eye contact, but let your gaze shift away as you think about what they have said. Nod and smile when you agree; ask questions that invite the speaker to expand upon what they've just said. Take the attitude of a learner and look for things you can discover.

Prime Your Attitudes

Contrary to popular belief, you are in control of your attitudes. While you can't control much of what happens to you, you *can* choose how you view the challenges of life. It's completely up to you whether you view a situation as basically hopeful or fundamentally hopeless. This attitude will largely determine whether you speak positive, affirming phrases to others or whether you become known as a pessimistic, gloomy wet blanket.

Paradise, while not denying the vicissitudes of life, is committed to promoting the positive. It's determined to infuse the environment with life, hope, and all things good. You build your home into a paradise by taking your attitudes under wing and shaping them for good. Here are some practices that can help:

- Speak positive affirmations aloud – When you choose to speak statements of positive worth to yourself, you are working to actively counter the myriad negative, destructive messages you have absorbed over decades of living in this rough world. These statements actually work to turn around your attitudes, but only if they are repeated many times each day. Adopt a specific list of positive affirmations, make a habit of repeating them up to 100 times a day, and watch your attitude toward your life improve!

- Whenever you come up with a negative statement, turn it around and make a counteractive, up-building, positive statement. Instead of waking up and thinking, "Oh, boy; here we go again. I dread just getting out of bed," say "Today is a gift that I'm going to enjoy to the hilt, just as soon as I stretch and fully wake up."

- Adopt a can-do spirit. Remember "The Little Engine That Could?" Instead of dwelling on difficulties, look for glimmers of hope in the situation and tell yourself, "I think I can." Give yourself permission to succeed.

- Practice forgiveness. You can only have a paradise in your home if you are free from grudges, harbored anger, and bitterness. Acknowledge your wounds; don't hide from them. Actively choose to forgive, to let go of the past wrong, drop it, and move forward in your life. Your home paradise is calling you to live in the Now, in what has been called, "the holy present."

Harness Your Emotions

Emotions are neither good nor bad; they simply are. What is positive or destructive is your response to your emotions. You may choose to dig deeply into that emotion, to feel it to the hilt, to know it fully. Just remember, however, that even the best emotions are fleeting. Eventually you'll resurface and find life going on without you.

Another possible response is to ignore a feeling. Let's say, one day you suddenly feel incredibly sad. Because you don't know why you're sad, you decide this feeling is not worth your time, so you just stuff it down deep inside and get on with your day. The trouble is, emotions may submit to you shoving them aside for the moment, but they never go away completely. That sadness will sit around moping deep inside you. Eventually, it will resurface, bringing friends and with even greater urgency than before. If at all possible, it's better to deal with your emotions when at the time surface.

Another possible response is simply to drown it out by sheer level of distraction. If you're busy, double your level of activity. Increase your sheer busy-ness until you have no space for thought; you drop dead-tired into bed at night and the next morning you charge immediately into your day, full-speed ahead. Yes, you can shove your feelings aside if you want, but if you don't run yourself into the ground first, the emotion that started the feeding frenzy will still be there, hanging out, waiting.

The most realistic way to live with your emotions is to:

- Acknowledge that they exist (don't ignore them). Tell yourself, "I feel _____," articulating how you feel at the moment, to the best of your ability.

- Decide when you're going to delve fully into that emotion and explore all that it means. If you're not busy, you can give yourself 30 minutes right then. If, however, you're in the middle of a busy work day (and who isn't?) you will want to set aside some time later – a specific time, mind you – to get alone in private, to face this emotion, and to deal with its implications.

- Tell yourself lovingly what you've chosen to do, then turn to your next activity.

- When you are able to deal with your emotion, get alone and remind yourself how you were feeling earlier. Allow yourself to experience the emotion fully, from every angle. Choose how you want to express your emotion to yourself (laughing, crying, singing, shouting, whispering, dancing, writing, etc.)

- Ask yourself, "What now?" and choose where you want to go from here. Can you let the emotion go and move forward at this point? Do you need to grieve? Vent? Forgive someone? Take action? Respond with your creative energies?

- Plan anything that needs to be planned. Then give yourself permission to let go – at least for now – and move on.

Chapter 6: Ahh, It Smells Like Paradise!

The principle is pretty simple. If your home smells good, you feel good. If it smells like garbage, you feel like garbage. Your family and your visitors will all love to come to your house if it smells pleasant. The best defense against a smelly house is to keep it clean. Beyond that, this chapter will give you a host of ideas for using scented candles, essential oils, and potpourri to enhance the ambiance of your home.

Kitchen Aromas

Baking just before guests arrive will make them feel welcome. Keep some cookie dough in the freezer; then place a few in the oven, ready to pull out about the time the doorbell rings. Another mouthwatering aroma is the smell of fresh bread. You can always keep some frozen bread dough on hand to pop in the oven and fill that the house with fresh bread scent.

Odor Neutralizers

If you were to sniff **baking soda** (I would be careful about sniffing too hard) you would not smell much. You probably know about the tradition of putting a box of baking soda in the refrigerator to absorb odors. It works because baking soda soaks up and neutralizes bad smells.

Vinegar has an acrid scent that can be off-putting for some people. The thing about vinegar is that it does have that initial salad dressing smell, but as it sits, it absorbs other, more distasteful scents and leaves a "nothing" smell in its place. The vinegar smell dissipates in 30 minutes.

Place some baking soda or vinegar in small dishes and set them in areas out of the way of children and pets. I keep a small bowl of vinegar in my bathroom and it fends on the litter box smell, among other odors. This won't add scent to your home, but it will neutralize less attractive smells.

Citrus Air Freshening

Citrus fruits give off a lovely clean scent that is pleasing to the senses. Cut a lemon or orange in half. Juice it, then sprinkle about one tablespoon of **salt** on the inside of the peel along with a few **whole cloves**. Place them in a bowl and leave them around the house where pets and children cannot reach them. The salt enhances the scent and keeps the skins from quickly rotting. Once they stop giving off their pleasant aroma, it is time to throw the peels away and start with a new batch.

Air Vent Fresheners

You know those cute little deodorizers you clip onto the vents in your car? You can use them in your house, too. Just clip them onto the louvers of your air vents. The air passing through the vents will push the scent out into the rooms and get rid of any stale air.

Scent Your Home With Dryer Sheets

Dryer sheets come in a variety of scents that can be used to refresh the entire house. Pop off the cover of a heating vent, lay a dryer sheet over the back side of the vent, and pop it back on. The heated air in the winter will flow through the dryer sheet, which is designed to be heat-activated, and will invisibly scent the room. While manufacturers make no claims to this effect, dryer sheets may also trap and prevent floating debris from entering both the room and your lungs as you inhale.

Essential Oils

Essential oils are scents extracted from plants by a distillation method. Essential oils are much more potent than fragrance oils, which are usually synthetic in nature. Essential oils are always preferable, as they are stronger in scent and natural. Here are a few ways they can be used to freshen all areas of your home.

Light bulbs – I must have twenty little bottles of essential oils in a variety of different scents. These come in very handy to scent my house. While a lamp is turned off and the bulb is cool, place a drop of a fragrant essential oil on the light bulb. When you turn the lamp on, the essential oil will grow warm and dissipate the scent into the environment.

Cotton balls – Another option is to lightly soak a cotton ball in a couple drops of essential oil that have been diluted in mineral oil and place it on a small dish. Set this dish in an out-of-the way spot and it will continue to scent your home for up to a week. I set the dish on top of the books in my living room bookshelf. It keeps the room smelling lovely.

Furnace filter – When you change your furnace filter, scatter 10 drops of your favorite essential oil on the fresh filter before you pop it into the furnace. The oils will scent the home for quite a long time and will circulate through the entire house.

Vacuum cleaner – Place some essential oil on a few cotton balls and place them in the bag of your vacuum cleaner. If you have a bagless type, sprinkle a handful of drops in the chamber where dirt collects. If you have a filter – washable or disposable – place a few drops there. The next time you vacuum, the scent will permeate the air.

The commode and toilet paper – It is essential that your bathroom smell fresh and clean for your family and for visitors when they call. There are two ways you can use essential oils to keep your toilet area smelling fresh and clean. The first way is to drop a few drops of an essential oils into your toilet bowl. Eucalyptus and tea tree oil have an antiseptic scent that makes the toilet feel clean and fresh. You can also use other oils, like lavender or citrus.

The second way to freshen your entire bathroom is to place two drops of an essential oil on the inside of the cardboard toilet paper roll. Each time someone reaches for toilet paper, it will release the scent into the room.

Mattress – Mix ½ cup baking soda with 12 drops of essential oil in a glass bowl. Set aside and let the concoction dry for about ½ hour. Sprinkle on your mattress and rub it in with your hands. Let it sit one hour and vacuum the baking soda off. It will leave your mattress smelling fresh and airy for your family members or for overnight visitors. The best essential oil to use for this is lavender. Lavender is relaxing in nature and promotes sound sleep.

Fireplace Freshener – It might sound funny to use essential oils in the fireplace, but when visitors come over on a cold night and you light it up, you will see that it lends a very cozy and pleasant atmosphere to the room. Four drops of either pine or sage essential oil on the logs in the fireplace, will make for a delightful-smelling blaze. Mint also works pretty well, too, and is great for after dinner, as it tends to settle the stomach.

Make Your Own Bamboo Diffuser

You have seen those pretty bamboo diffusers with a colorful glass container with bamboo sticks poking up from the opening. The scented liquid in the bottle soaks in and travels up the bamboo to infuse your home with a lovely scent. They can be quite expensive, but you don't have to spend a lot of money to get a heavenly scent. Here's how you can make your own scent diffuser, for a fraction of the retail price.

You start with a **bottle** of any size that has a fairly small opening. Select something you will enjoy looking at. For the fragrance, you can use a citrus-scented cleaning solution, you can buy commercial fragrance blends, or you can make your own, using any essential oil. Lavender or lilac is always nice, but if you want something a little stronger, let me suggest rose or frankincense.

Combine seven to 10 drops of a favorite essential oil in one cup of mineral oil and in the diffuser bottle.

For infuser rods, use <u>bamboo shish-kabob skewers</u> and trim off the points with scissors. The skewers should be twice the height of the fragrance container, so if your jar is 8 inches tall, the skewers need to be 16 inches tall.

Microwave diffuser – Another way to diffuse scent throughout your home is to use a glass bowl and place about one to two cups of water in with one to nine drops of an essential oil. Place the bowl in the microwave and microwave on high for about three to five minutes, making sure it does not boil over or boil dry. When you open the microwave, the scent will diffuse all through your home.

Spray diffuser – In a glass bowl mix one tablespoon of baking soda with two to three drops of an essential oil. I use a craft stick to mix it up and then just toss it away. Add this mixture to a plastic spray bottle and add 12 ounces of distilled water. Shake it up well and spray to cleanse the air in the home.

Potpourri – Potpourri has been used throughout the centuries to make the home smell delightfully habitable. Centuries ago, people did not have indoor sewer systems. Everything would end up in gutters in front of houses. Needless to say, this made for a rather odiferous atmosphere; the larger the city, the greater the stench. What people used in the Middle Ages to keep the outdoor smells at bay was to strew herbs, leaves, and aromatic flowers over the interior floors. As people walked across them, they would bruise and release their pleasant scent. In time, this became the potpourri we know today. Potpourri is now made out of pretty dried flowers, leaves, cones, nuts and even ribbons and other fabric.

Potpourri is made from either botanicals – things that have been alive but are now dried – or non-botanicals. Botanicals may include:

- dry flowers
- dried leaves
- nuts or acorns
- pine cones
- dried grasses
- berries like juniper or bittersweet
- cinnamon (comes from bark of a tree)
- whole cloves
- citrus rinds
- dried fruits, such as apples
- twigs and bark from deciduous trees

Non-Botanicals include:

- stones
- sea glass

- fabric pieces
- torn paper
- pieces of pretty ribbon
- glass beads

The botanicals make the potpourri smell good and the non-botanicals just make it pleasing to look at.

Wet Potpourri

Wet potpourri is also called hot liquid potpourri. This type of potpourri only utilizes botanical substances. Prepare it in a simmering saucepan or purchase a small two-serving Crock-Pot. All you have to do is make sure there is enough water in the container to keep the potpourri wet. Every once in a while, I pass by and drop in a little more liquid. Keep the Crock-Pot temperature on low. For the stovetop form of potpourri, keep the mixture barely bubbling.

The following are some recipes for wet potpourri that will delight your family and visitors:

Citrus and Spice – lice up one orange, peel and all in flat slices. Do the same with one lemon. Place the sliced fruit in a pan or crock pot with water and add two small cinnamon sticks, four whole cloves and one bay leaf.

Cranberry Spice – Slice up an orange and add one cup whole cranberries to the water in the sauce pan or crock pot. Add two cinnamon sticks and one tablespoon of whole cloves.

Minty Fresh – Place three to four sprigs of mint in water in the sauce pan or crock pot and add two drops of peppermint oil.

Cinnamon Buns – Place two cinnamon sticks, one teaspoon vanilla extract, one teaspoon vanilla extract and some powdered nutmeg in water or apple cider and boil.

Apple Pie – Slice two apples flat along with peels and place in water. Add two cinnamon sticks, the juice of one lemon and one teaspoon vanilla extract.

Kitchen Freshening Simmer – Cut up one lemon and place in water with one tablespoon vanilla extract and three sprigs of rosemary.

Fresh and Clean – Cut up one lemon and place it in water and add one cup dried eucalyptus leaves or two to 5 drops of eucalyptus oil and one teaspoon vanilla extract.

Minty Lime – Cut up two limes and add to water along with two springs of mint and ½ teaspoon peppermint extract.

Holiday Mix – Place two cinnamon sticks in water with two twigs of fresh pine needles. Add two drops of pine or peppermint essential oil.

Gingerbread Simmer – Peel and slice 10 pieces of fresh ginger and add to water with one cinnamon stick and one teaspoon vanilla extract.

Coffee – The coffee drinker will love this one. Grind two tablespoons coffee beans and add to the water with a tablespoon of dried orange peel and one teaspoon vanilla extract.

Dry Potpourri

Place your dry potpourri in pretty glass bowls. If you don't want kids or pets to get into them, place a circle of nylon netting over the opening of the bowl and secure with a rubber band. Cover the rubber band with a ¼ inch silk ribbon, hot gluing it on. I make my potpourri in pint jars, put the netting over top and top with a screw on rim and seal. When I want to use the potpourri, I just take the seal off and replace the rim.

The nice thing about potpourri is that it is visually attractive as well as scent attractive. If the scent starts to fade, you just add more essential oils and either shake it up (in the jar) or mix it up in the bowl. Use the non-botanical items to make your potpourri look attractive. I cut little one-inch squares of pretty fabric or scrapbook paper, and ½ to one inch lengths of pretty ribbon to add. I also use sea glass and stones on occasion just to make it look beautiful in the jar. These have to be removed before adding more scent and shaking the jar, but you can put them right back in afterwards. Seashells also make the potpourri more attractive.

When you make potpourri, you must use a fixative. This is a substance that grabs on to the essential oils you put in the potpourri and holds on to them for a time. If you do not use a fixative, your scent will only last a few days. Use the following fixatives:

- Orris root
- Oak moss
- Staghorn moss
- Fiberfix

Orris root is the chopped or powdered root from a type of iris; it has a slight scent on its own. Oak moss and Staghorn moss are both dried and have no scent. Fiberfix is a synthetic mix that takes on the scent of the oils.

When using Orris root, Oak moss or Staghorn moss, add about one to two tablespoons per cups of potpourri. If you make three cups of potpourri you would add three to six tablespoons of the fixative. When using Fiberfix you must first mix the substance with the fragrant oils and wait about two hours for the Fiberfix to marinate. This will support about five pounds of potpourri. You can use one to two drops of essential oil per cup of finished potpourri.

The following are some of my favorite dry potpourri mixes:

Old Thyme Lavender

1 cup dried lavender flowers

½ cup dry pink dianthus (small carnation) flowers

½ cup dry bee balm flowers

¼ cup dried lambs ear leaves

¼ cup dried thyme

2 tablespoons orris root

5 drops lavender oil

Citrus

½ cup dried lemon verbena

½ cup dried lemon balm

½ cup dried lemon thyme

½ cup dried calendula petals

¼ cup dried chamomile flower

2 tablespoons dried lemon, lime or orange rind

5 drops lemon oil or bergamot oil

Apple

1 cup dried apples with peels on

½ cup crushed cinnamon

12 whole cloves

1 cup dried lambs ear leaves

½ cup dried berries

2 to 4 drops cinnamon oil

Orange Spice

1 cup bee balm or bergamot flowers

1 cup citrus scented geranium leaves

1 cup lemon balm

¼ cup dried crushed orange peel

5 crushed star anise pods

2 crushed cinnamon sticks

six whole cloves

5 drops orange oil

Pine

1 cup small pine cones (hemlock cones are best)

1 cup dried pine needles

½ cup cedar shavings

½ cup dried bittersweet berries or juniper berries

2 to three drops pine oil

Victorian Rose

1 cup dried rose petals (stay away from white or light yellow roses because they turn brown)

½ cup lavender flowers

1 cup dried red or pink dianthus flowers

1 cup dried lambs ear leaves

5 to six drops rose oil or three drops rose oil and 2 drops lavender oil

Asian Flavor

1 cup dried rose petals

1 cup dried jasmine flower petals

½ cup dried basil leaves

¼ cup dried gingerroot chopped

2 crushed star anise

1 teaspoon cumin seed

2 to three drops rose oil

2 to 3 drops jasmine flower oil

Other Scents

Eucalyptus – Treatment Eucalyptus has a strong scent that some might say is antiseptic. It tends to clear the sinuses. I happen to love the smell, even when I don't have a stuffy head cold. That said, hanging a sprig of eucalyptus in or near the shower where it won't get wet, will scent the bathroom when you take a shower. The steam releases the oils into the room. It can definitely clear your head in the morning, as well as making the room smell very pleasant.

Citrus peels – The garbage disposal is easily a major source of offensive household odors. Nothing is worse than anticipating an at-home feeling after a long day away, only to be walloped by a garbagy malodor as you enter your kitchen. It's even worse when you realize the stench is coming from your sink.

Eat an orange or cook with a lemon and toss the peels in your garbage disposal to freshen it. I keep some peels in zip-lock bags in the refrigerator or freezer and use them throughout the week. I never keep them longer than four days in the refrigerator but find that they seem to keep their freshness as long as they stay cold. If you freeze fruit rinds, they last longer and it doesn't hurt to put them down the garbage disposal while frozen. Just run that disposal and get rid of the nasty smell.

The Vinegar Fix – Vinegar will also deodorize your garbage disposal. Throw a few ice cubes in along with a squirt or two of white or apple cider vinegar and churn away. The ice cubes will dislodge anything stuck to the blades and the vinegar will kill the germs and help break down greasy buildup.

You now have a host of practical suggestions you can use to refresh the fragrances of your home. Feel free to experiment with potpourris – both dry and wet, essential oils, even dryer sheets to create aromas that make your home smell like paradise.

Chapter 7: Preserve Your Fabrics

Your home is full of all types of fabrics, from the clothing on your back to the carpet on your floor. Furnishings are often made of fabric, your bed, curtains, towels, table linens, and dish cloths all fabrics that require care to last long and make your house the paradise it deserves to be. This chapter will help you to take care of all those fabrics and keep them in good shape for many years to come.

Clothing

Clothing is expensive and you want it to look its best. Many times clothing will fade and start looking worn and tattered after only a few washes. Some clothing cannot be washed in a regular washing machine but must be dry cleaned. Don't even try to wash it yourself because it rarely comes out all right. Suits get wrinkled beyond repair and the fabric becomes shiny. Some clothing is easily washed by hand in a mild soap. Check the label on the clothing to see the best way to handle washing a garment. If it says don't wring, do not wring it out or the garment will be stretched out of shape. If the tag says dry flat, do not hang it because it will stretch into strange shapes and never look right again.

For clothes that can be cleaned using a washer and dryer, always pull them out of the dryer as soon as possible to minimize the appearance of wrinkles. Hang up cotton and synthetic clothing and fold knits and T-shirts to be placed in a drawer.

Here are a few tips on how to keep clothing looking its best:

- Always wash new clothing before you wear it. When you do, add ¼ cup salt to the washer; this will protect the color and slow its fading. Sea salt or regular table salt both work fine.

- Read the labels on your clothes before you wash them. If a label says to use cold water, never use hot water. If it says to hand wash, don't put it in the washing machine.

- Turn clothing inside out before washing. This is the part that is against your skin and collects dead cells; washing wrong-side out makes it easy for those cells to wash away while the fabric is being cleaned. It also protects buttons and ornaments from catching on the agitator during the spin cycle and ripping off sequins, and other bling.

- Invest in mesh bags for items with lace or spaghetti straps that easily get tangled around the agitator or other clothes.

- Clothing launders best in cold water. The colors will not fade or run and wrinkles will not set in.

- Take care of stains right away, even while wearing the garment. The longer a stain sets, the harder it will be to get out. Dab stains with absorbent cloths instead of rubbing the fibers out of shape. Use cold water, never warm, to get rid of stains and presoak the garment immediately when taking it off.

- While convenient, the dryer does tend to damage the fibers of your clothes over time. Some fibers will shrink. It is always best to line-dry clothing with a few exceptions. Jeans, PJs and underwear would be a few. Jeans do much better in the dryer anyway.

Carpet/rugs

Carpet and rugs can help your home's ambience. They add to the comfort level and absorb sound, giving you and oasis of peace. Area rugs can create a focal point, as well as a comfy place to sit on the floor. However, they can also be a little expensive. All the better reason to take good care of them, so they will last for years. Here are a few ways to freshen and clean your carpets and rugs:

Carpet Freshener

No one likes a stinky carpet. If you have kids and pets, you know that carpets can harbor distasteful smells for a long time. Baking soda not only soaks up smells in your refrigerator, it is also safe to use on your rugs. Just sprinkle some on the carpet and let it set for five to 10 minutes before you vacuum it up. The results: a fresher-smelling room. Don't go too wild with your sprinkling or you'll have a real mess on your hands. Just sprinkle enough that you know it is there.

Carpet Stain Remover

Avoid installing light- to medium-colored carpet if you have kids and pets. I have learned my lesson; let's leave it at that. Even dark carpet shows up some dirt and stains. At any rate, you'll need these hacks if you have any carpet in your home.

As with any stain remover, you'll want to test these solutions before using them on a stain. Because some types of carpet – especially wool – may not respond well, you will want to test these remedies in an inconspicuous corner before using a solution in the middle of the room.

I am now an expert at getting stains out of carpet – after all, I have the carpet I warned you about. This is how I do it. Combine white vinegar and distilled water in equal parts in a spray bottle. Every time you get a stain on your carpet, first blot off what you can with a paper towel. Then spray it. Let this solution rest on the carpet for 10 minutes or so, then take a scrub brush dipped in tap water and scrub the spot. Blot the spot again and the stain should lift out, unless it is one of those stubborn stains you encounter occasionally. But I have a solution – or two – for even those recalcitrant stains.

Wine Spills on Carpet – Wine spills on carpet are easy to clean up, so rather than telling your guests the wine can't go into a carpeted area, keep some shaving cream on hand. When a spill occurs, take a paper towel and blot up as much as possible. To blot means to press down, but *not* to rub. Once you have taken up most of the liquid, spray shaving cream on the spot, let it set for a few minutes and start blotting again. The stain should come right up.

Vacuum your rugs and carpets at least once a week. Dirt can actually cut into carpet fibers, causing it to deteriorate more quickly, so you'll want to keep on top of it, especially in high-traffic areas.

Upholstery Maintenance

It is important to keep upholstered furniture looking its best for that lived-in-paradise look. Clean furniture makes a house feel so very wonderful. Here are a few ways to clean and maintain your upholstery.

Use your vacuum cleaner attachments to clean your upholstery at least once a month. The long flat wand will get dirt and grime out of the cracks of the seats and around inset buttons while the brush will get grime and dust off the flat surfaces of the cushions and underneath the furniture (yes, tip it back and vacuum the underside). If your upholstered furniture has not been sprayed with a soil retardant, purchase some in a spray can and treat your upholstery each six months, after you've cleaned it . If you can rotate and flip the cushions, do so at least four times a year. This will help them retain their shape. Use white paper towels or soft white cloths to dab up spills and stains. Avoid using colored towels, because they may bleed and transfer color to the upholstery.

Upholstery is coded for proper maintenance, as follows:

- W – means vacuum and light dusting required. A non-solvent detergent can be used.

- S – means a light dusting and treatment with a combination of spot cleaner is possible. Dry cleaning by a professional is required.

- S/W – a combination of water and solvent must be used.

Upholstery Stain Cleaner – When your upholstery is stained, first blot the stain with a soft cloth laid atop the stain. Do not rub; you want to absorb liquid before it can soak down into the fibers. Anything that soaks into the upholstery will call for a little extra work.

To make an upholstery stain cleaner, mix 1/2 cup of cornstarch with 1/2 cup baking soda in a bowl. Add just enough water to form a paste. Apply the paste to the stain and leave it alone until it dries. It is important to cover the stain with the paste, but don't pile it on; you want it to dry in thirty minutes to an hour.

After drying, carefully scrape off the paste with a dull knife or a spatula. The stain should come up along with it. Vacuum up any remaining debris.

Bedding

Mattress – A comfortable bed is a paradise all its own. To sustain the life of your mattress, I recommend using a mattress cover to protect the fabric. A periodic vacuum session with an upholstery brush will also extend the life of your mattress. Mattresses should also be flipped twice a year, first from side to side and then from foot to head. Like rotating your tires, flipping your mattress will even the wear and make it last much longer.

Sheets should be laundered at least once a week. Use warm water instead of hot, since hot water tends to break and bend fibers. Colored pillowcases should be washed inside out to minimize the fading of colors. Tumble your sheets dry, removing them immediately to prevent wrinkles. You also can hang sheets outside on the line to dry and absorb the fresh smell of the great outdoors, but they will be softer if you use a dryer. The next time you buy sheets, remember that thread count makes all the difference in the world. A higher thread count feels more luxurious.

Pillows should be covered by zippered pillow protectors. These fabric bags repel liquids and protect the pillow from stains. We all drool at night, so this will protect your pillows from moisture and germs. In addition, you will want to use a pillowcase for more protection and for your own comfort. Synthetic and down pillows are often machine washable, but check your care label to be sure. Just pop it in the washer and transfer to the dryer. If your pillows come out of the dryer misshapen, it's an indication the time has come to buy a new one.

Wash your pillows at least twice a year, the protector four times a year and pillowcases whenever you wash your sheets. You can also warm your pillows in the dryer at any time to get rid of dust mites and to fluff them up. To fluff up pillows, set the dryer on low heat and place two or three tennis balls in white tube socks and tie them shut. Add these to the dryer with the pillows and let them tumble away.

Blankets should be washed periodically, but not necessarily as often as sheets. I like to wash mine every month. The bedspread may or may not be washable; just read the care label before proceeding. Some bedspreads require professional cleaning;, I steer clear of them. My quilts and blankets are all machine-washable and dryable.

It never feels nice to climb into a rumpled bed at night. Make your bed every morning; make it part of your morning ritual. Pull the wrinkles out of the bottom sheet and reposition the top sheet, the blanket, and the bedspread.

You won't believe how much more comfortable it is to hop into a straightened bed. I used to think, "Why should I make my bed when I will be back here messing it up in a few hours?" However, it makes a world of difference when you turn down the neat covers and climb in a bed that isn't askew. Trust me; you'll sleep better.

Table Linens

Fabric tablecloths are a real luxury in today's world. Most people slap place mats or plastic tablecloths on the table and let it go at that. A fabric tablecloth exudes richness and it isn't very hard to keep them clean, either. Just use a gentle detergent on fabric tablecloths to keep them looking great.

It is best to run tablecloths through the rinse cycle twice, just to make sure all the soap has been removed. Never use bleach with <u>linen</u> because it may discolor. Some linen-tablecloths can be dried in the dryer, but it is better to hang them on a line outside and iron the tablecloth while it is barely damp, using medium-high heat. Tablecloths that are 100% <u>cotton</u> should be ironed on the high setting. <u>Polyester</u> tablecloths are easily washed with cool water under a regular setting for both washer and dryer. Launder no more than two tablecloths at a time, because of their weight.

<u>Organza</u> should be washed on the delicate cycle or hand washed. Hang it to dry or use a low setting on the dryer and remove the cloth before it is completely dry. <u>Satin</u> requires cold water on the delicate cycle with regular laundry detergent. Dry on low heat and remove immediately. <u>Lace</u> tablecloths should be hand-washed in cold water with mild detergent. Be careful not to scrub too hard or you run the risk of tearing the lace or pulling the pattern out of shape. Gently squeeze dry or fold into a big bath towel and squeeze dry gently. Hang to dry the rest of the way.

To store tablecloths, wrap them around a cardboard tube or a pool noodle so they do not wrinkle. You can also fold them in thirds and drape them over a suit hanger.

Curtains And Drapes

Always check for cleaning instructions on labels attached to your curtains and drapery. I remember my father once decided to wash our drapes in the washing machine. We itched for months afterwards, because they were made of fiberglass. Little fiberglass fragments embedded in the washer were transferred to our clothing whenever it was washed, for what seemed like forever. We were miserable, but the drapes actually looked pretty good!

Most lined drapes must be dry cleaned to prevent the lining from shrinking and puckering the drapes, ruining them forever. Silk, polished cotton, and wool drapes must also be dry cleaned.

There is a way to clean drapes without putting them in the washer, provided that they do not have any stains. You can use your vacuum cleaner to remove the dust and grime. Use a handheld vacuum, placing a nylon knee-high sock over the hose. Begin at the top, standing on a stepstool or ladder as needed, and vacuum your way down through all the folds to the bottom hem. You may need to remove the sock periodically to shake out captured debris into a garbage bag.

Sheers are usually washable. Check the label first. If they lack a label, use the gentle cycle and wash in warm water, using a gentle detergent. Air dry or dry them under low heat for twenty minutes, removing immediately, and rehanging without delay, in order to prevent wrinkles from setting in.

Cotton curtains are easily laundered in warm water and tumbled dry on a low temperature setting. They may need to be ironed, preferably with steam, before hanging back in the window.

Fabric Lampshades

Fabric lampshades can become dingy and stained over time. They also collect pet hair like crazy! While they may really need a good cleaning, fabric lampshades can be tricky to clean. Water can leave permanent marks and dust tends to bury itself tenaciously within the fibers of the fabric. That's not to say the situation is hopeless, however.

Begin by using the brush attachment on your vacuum to suck off dust and pet hair. If your shade is pleated, use the flat wand attachment to get in all the nooks and crannies. If that doesn't take care of everything, apply an adhesive roller, the kind used to remove pet hair from clothing, to the lampshade. It should effectively pick up the dust and dirt..

Fabric lampshades can be cleaned with water and a gentle soap, just as long as the fabric is not backed by paper! Newer lampshades are plastic-lined, so they can tolerate the immersion.

For this process, remove the lampshade from its base. Fill a tub or large basin with soapy water and immerse the lampshade. Use a soft brush to gently remove tough dirt. Rinse the shade after cleaning and hang it up to dry.

With lampshades that cannot be immersed, dilute a small amount of laundry detergent in a spray bottle with plenty of water. It should suds up when shaken. Remove the lampshade and place it on a plastic surface – a countertop, tablecloth or plastic drop cloth will do. Spray a small area of the lampshade beginning at the top. If the shade is not too fragile to tolerate it, use a toothbrush to scrub problem areas, including existing water stains.

Blot the area with dry cloths to pull out as much moisture, grime, and staining before moving to the next spot. Work from top to bottom and all the way around. Next, pour out the detergent mixture and rinse the bottle well. Fill with two tablespoons of white vinegar and about one cup of warm water. Spray the lampshade lightly all the way around and blot with another clean dry towel. Set the lampshade aside to dry completely before returning it to its place atop your favorite lamp.

Stain-Removal From Fabrics In Your Home

Wax melted into fabric– Place a paper towel over the wax and press with a hot iron on low to medium heat. A paper bag will also work because it will absorb the wax just like the paper towel.

Grease stains – Dish detergent formulated to get rid of grease works wonders on fabric grease stains. Squirt a tiny bit of detergent on the stain and massage gently with a white absorbent cloth or a bath towel. Rinse carefully with warm water.

Blood – Hydrogen peroxide dabbed on blood stains will get them out. Always test the fabric in an inconspicuous place before applying hydrogen peroxide to the stain.

Magic markers – Use rubbing alcohol to dab out marker stains.

Ink stains – Ink may come out with a paste made from milk and cornstarch. Applied and leave it on the stain for two hours before wiping it off. An alternative paste is made using ¼ teaspoon of cream of tartar and one teaspoon of hydrogen peroxide.

Pet Urine – Try wetting a paper towel with club soda to blot up pet urine and get rid of the smell.

When you protect the fabrics in the house and clean them frequently, you are preparing a paradise oasis for you, your family, and your visitors to enjoy. Now, let's move on to discuss how the rest of your possessions can contribute to your home paradise.

Chapter 8: The Stuff That Makes Up Paradise

The way you take care of your possessions has a huge impact on the quality of your home paradise Too much stuff all around can make a home feel cluttered and claustrophobic. In contrast, paradise should feel unrestrained and airy, so it is important to keep the things you own in check.

One way to keep your possessions under control is by choosing to get rid of something whenever you choose to buy a related item. Every time I buy a pair of shoes, I get rid of a pair; this prevents me from amassing hundreds of shoes that I never wear. You can do this with just about any item in your home: books, kitchen utensils, pots and pans, jewelry, decorative ornaments, to name a few. Keep just what you need and avoid unnecessary excess.

It's also important to take care of what you do have. Launder your clothing and either hang it up or put it in drawers to reduce the risk of damage. Dust your books periodically and display them neatly on shelves. Clean kitchen utensils and store them away. Keep pots and pans sparkling and store them by hanging to keep them from getting warped or scratched. Clean your jewelry on a regular basis and keep it in a special box or drawer so that nothing gets lost. Dust your decorative ornaments frequently to keep them looking their best.

If you don't have a lot of possessions, it is much easier to take care of what you do have. Purge your stuff on a yearly basis. Take an item in your hands and ask yourself if you really need it. If you do, keep it and put it away. If you aren't sure or know you don't need it anymore, donate it or get rid of it.

Here are the major categories of stuff that can get out of hand from time to time, along with helpful strategies for keeping them under your control:

Toys

Toys are a constant source of clutter, but there are ways to contain them. Designate a play area in your home that is out of the way of the living area Put down a brightly colored rug to designate that place for toys. Store toys in plastic bins, a toy box or in baskets around the edge of the play area.

Your kids do not need every toy they own in the space at the same time. Rotate the toys, leaving just enough to keep them busy in the area, while the rest are hidden in a closet or in a shallow tub under their beds. Every other week rotate some stored toys into the play area and stash some that have been out for a while.

You can also put toys on open bookshelves that mark the perimeter of the play area; just make sure these shelves are anchored to the ceiling or each other to prevent them from falling if climbed upon.

Books, DVDs And CDs

Books lying flat on a coffee table take up too much room and tend to clutter the area. Store all books on a bookshelf to keep them looking tidy, never laying on a flat surface. E-readers are a great way to handle books, newspapers, and magazines. Instead of paper lying around in the way, you have the small e-reader with which to enjoy them. Most e-readers hold many different publications at one time, which can greatly reduce your paper clutter. In most cases, e-books and e-subscriptions are much cheaper than the paper versions, mainly because they include no mailing or printing fees. Kindle and Nook are the most popular e-readers, but there are others that also work moderately well. One of the best things about e-publications is that you can read documents on your computer and your smartphone, as well as on a dedicated e-reader.

Store DVDs and CDs, if you still use them, in towers made for that purpose or in a bookcase. A hollow ottoman with a lid is another good place to stash them, or baskets under a coffee table.

MP3 players store about 1,500 songs, which gives you the equivalent of around 150 CDs. You can play MP3s on other devices as well, so this format is ideal.

Most computers come with software that will rip music to your computer, but the programs are minimal. There are other programs out there that are either freeware or may cost a bit of money, but they have better tools and include the ability to store music in multiple formats:

- Fairstar's CD Ripper is a good and easy tool to use.

- Exact Audio Copy is good at filling in spots where a CD might be scratched.

- CDex Q is a free option for creating MP3s.

If you would rather have a service rip your CDs for you, there are several options. The process is fairly simple. You just ship off your CDs and they come back in any format you wish. Here are a few of the most well-known services:

- MusicShifter is a reputable service that will transfer several CDs free, depending on how many you are having processed.

- Dmp3 Digital transfers music from CDs to any number of formats.

- Riptopia performs standard ripping services.

Most of these services charge $1 per CD (make sure it isn't $1 per minute) and they provide spindles on which to store your CDs and a box in which to send them. You get your CDs back in a few days along with digital files.

DVDs are becoming a thing of the past. It is so easy to download movies from a cable provider or to subscribe to Netflix, Hulu or other services, that few DVDs are needed. You can now take all your old DVDs and transcribe them into your computer storage. Then you can watch them directly on your computer or you can hook your computer up to your television for viewing on a larger screen.

Some good video transcoders are:

- Handbrake
- Wondershare
- Zencoder from Brightcove
- Wowza
- MPEG Streamclip
- Super from eRightSoft

Some of these are free while others begin with free trials followed by required subscription. You can store your movies on the cloud, on your computer, and on other devices.

Jewelry

Jewelry can be stored in jewelry boxes and placed in dresser drawers, but you can also hang necklaces and bracelets from hooks or pegs on the wall. A tie rack attached to a wall of your closet can organize your jewelry neatly and accessibly, while keeping everything out of the way.

Photos

Storing your photos on a flash drive, an external hard drive, on your computer, or on the cloud is quite simple. You can scan and store your photos yourself, or you can send them to a service that will scan the images for you. Scanning items yourself does take time, but it will save you some money if funds are tight.

I also recommend saving your photos on the cloud, to avoid losing them. After scanning them, you can always give the paper photos to family members. The best thing about storing photos digitally is that they are easy to share with friends and family members; all it takes is sending a text or email, or posting on the internet.

If you look for a photo service to store your photos on the cloud, there are several things to consider:

- Space – Make sure you get plenty of space for a low cost.
- Quality – make sure that the service does not compress photos. Compression can compromise the quality of your photos if not done

correctly. If a company compresses photos, look at a sample to ensure that the quality is clear and flawless.

- Ease of Use – You want to be able to easily access your photos. Make sure you can store images in whatever order you like. You should be able to store photos by date, by event or by some other tag.

- Security – While you want to be able to access your photos with ease, you also want to restrict access to individuals you have granted viewing permission. Password access is usually sufficient protection.

- Easy of Sharing – You want to be able to easily share your photos with others and post them on social media.

- Printability – You should have the ability to print photos either from your own printer or at a photo kiosk.

The following are some companies that store photos for you:

- Shutterfly – Shutterfly has a free service for storing photos. It has very simple tools that make photos easy to print and share. They also offer paid services for printing your photos on calendars, mugs or other promotional items.

- 500 Pixels – serves primarily professional photographers. You can sort photos into albums, or stories for events. If you go to someone's wedding and take pictures there, you can store them in a story form that the wedding party can access and select photos for purchase. There is a free version of this software, but the paid subscription includes all sorts of lovely bells and whistles.

- Photobucket – is a service that offers a whole two gigabyte of storage for a fee. This service has great editing tools that anyone can figure out.

- Flickr – has a large selection of tools to work with. You get one terabyte of space free, as long as you can tolerate looking at ads. Viewing, editing, and downloading photos are all very easy.

- Facebook – Facebook offers you the ability to edit photos and create albums. The biggest problem with this service is that you have to fit your photos into their parameters of 720 by 960 pixels. They do compress photos, but most of the time the images come out looking pretty good.

- Google+ – Google plus uses some of the same features as Picasso Image Editing. It includes an extensive set of filters and tools for easily cropping and editing your photos.

Chapter 9: Basic Home Maintenance

Just like your car needs its oil changed every so often, your house needs certain maintenance activities to keep it in tip-top condition. Leaky faucets, smelly kitchen appliances, dusty ducts and clogged sinks do not a paradise make.

The following are some things you can do to make your home run smoothly inside and out:

Garbage Disposal – Never put cooked pasta, potato skins, rice, eggshells, celery, onion peels or other fibrous foods down the disposal. These things can wrap around the blades or clog up the drain. Avoid putting grease in the garbage disposal because it can also clog up the drain.

To sharpen the blades and make the disposal smell pleasant, make ice cubes from white vinegar. Put four or five of them in the disposal, turn on the water and run them through. This will dislodge any debris in the blades, sharpen them and make it smell better. Do this once every month.

Refrigerator Coils – Coils need to be vacuumed at least twice a year and more often if you have pets. without cleaning, the coils will utilize more energy to cool the refrigerator. You can save more than $100 a year just by performing this minor maintenance task. Find the coils on the backside of the refrigerator and use both the brush and the flat tube attachment of your vacuum to perform the task. For safety's sake, unplug the refrigerator while you clean the coils.

Coffee Maker – Coffee Makers can get a little dirty from time to time and this affects the flavor. It is very easy to clean the coffee maker. First, fill the reservoir with 1-part white vinegar and two parts cold tap water. Put it on brew and once it is finished draining into the pot, pour the hot solution back into the reservoir and run it through again.

Discard the vinegar solution and run another brew cycle with clear cold water. Discard that water and run another cycle with more fresh cold water. This will get rid of all debris in the coffee maker. Do this every other month or more frequently if you drink a lot of coffee.

Fire Extinguisher – If you have a fire extinguisher in your kitchen make sure it is an ABC class extinguisher. Do a check every month to make sure it is in working order. Your home paradise can burn down quickly without an extinguisher to stop a blaze before it grows out of hand. First, make sure the seals are intact. If not, get the extinguisher serviced or purchase another one.

Some home fire extinguishers include a pressure gauge. This tells you if it is ready to use. Some have a test button that will tell you if the pressure is good. Check the instructions to find out what pressure is suitable for operation. Also check for rusting, leakage, dents or a clogged nozzle. There should be a tag on the extinguisher. Always write the date of inspection on it so you remember when it was last performed.

Caulking – Caulking is the stuff that goes in the cracks around the tub and sink and around the bottom of tub and toilet. It keeps water from damaging your flooring and walls. Caulk can age and peel or crack, making it less effective. Check your caulk at least twice a year to prevent water damage to your home. If the caulk is failing, it needs to be removed and replaced. Carefully use a screwdriver to dig it out, if you can. Apply new caulk around the edge of the tub at the wall or surround line, at the floor line and around the faucet and spigot. Sinks should be caulked around the edges and around the faucets. The toilet is caulked around the floor line.

Dryer Vents – If you have your own clothes dryer, the vents need to be cleaned often. Clean the removable vent every time you dry a load. Twice a year you should use a vacuum to extract lint and dust from the area of the vent. Use a flat stick attachment to reach down to the depths of the machine. You can purchase a flexible brush that looks like a small chimney sweep brush. This needs to go through the vent and also the other direction through the hole in the wall to the outside to dislodge any debris. Clogging of the hose can slow the drying process and can also spark a fire in your home. I periodically remove the vent hose from the dryer and vacuum out underneath the dryer and inside the hose to the outside.

Water Heater – Water heaters are very expensive to replace. You can spend more than $1500 on a replacement, so it is important to keep them in good working order. Sediment can build up in a water heater, reducing its effectiveness. To minimize sediment buildup, at least once a year you should drain the water heater from the spigot at the bottom. Turn off the gas and electricity from the heater and then close off the valve that pours cold water into the tank. Attach a garden hose to the drain valve near the bottom and run it outside or to the nearest drain. Open the drain valve and let it drain completely. You may want to put the other end of the hose in a bucket to catch some of the drainage water and check for sediment in the heater. If you find any, drain the tank completely again after it's been refilled. After the process is completed, close the drain valve and turn the cold water back on.

Windows – Badly sealed windows can let up to 80% of winter heating and summer cooling go right out the window. Check the window caulking both inside and out for cracks and breaks; if necessary, replace it.

Gutters – Clogged gutters can leak water into a house. Debris that clogs gutters comes from many different sources. Falling leaves, grass driven by wind, and bird nests are some of the most common types of gutter debris. It is best to clean out gutters early in the spring and again before winter..

Outside Water Sources – Faucets that come from your home to the outside should have special treatment if you live in a cold climate. Water in those faucets can freeze and burst water pipes when the weather drops below freezing. Turn off the water valve inside to prevent water from going to the outside valve. Open the outside spigot to drain any water in the pipes. Turn the outside faucet off and leave it off during the winter. When turning it back on in the spring, turn the valve on from the inside before slowly opening up the outdoor faucet.

Garage Door Openers – Testing your garage door opener can make your property safety for kids and pets. Garage doors are built to stop closing if they hit anything of substance. Test this twice a year by placing a box or laundry hamper in the way of the door. Close the door and make sure it stops when it encounters any obstacle.

Emergency Kit – Every household should have an emergency kit. When I was a kid, we had one with candles, matches and candleholders in case we lost electric electricity. Today those candles can be replaced with safer battery-operated lanterns.

Your emergency kit should also include Band-Aids, anti-infection creams, scissors, a sharp knife, diapers if you have a young child, candy bars, and bottles of water. Place your emergency kit where you can easily reach in an emergency. I keep ours on a shelf at the bottom of the basement steps.

Furnace and Central Air– Change the HVAC filters on a regular basis. Some units require changing every month while others have less frequent requirements. Change it more often if you have pets, because their hair clogs the filters more quickly. Regularly filter replacement can prolong the life of your heating and cooling systems by avoiding the extra strain placed on the motors by forcing air through clogged filters.

Window Air Conditioners – Window conditioners need their filters cleaned at least before the season starts. Just remove the front grill and find the filmy filter. Shake it out to remove dust. Some filters are easily washed in soapy water. Air-dry before replacing into the unit. Window air conditioners should either be removed in the winter or wrapped with a tarp.

Smoke and Carbon Monoxide Detectors – Test detectors at least every six months. A good way to remember this is to watch for when the time changes. Change the batteries whether it needs to be done or not. This will ensure your family's safety for another half year.

Your home can remain a personal paradise by observing these few maintenance checks every year. They will keep your kids, yourself, your pets, and your visitors safe and will keep your home in good working condition for years to come.

Chapter 10: A Pet's Paradise

Pets are definitely a part of the family and you want them to feel that your home is a paradise for them as well as for the humans in your house. Dogs, cats and other pets are an integral part of the household. They give us joy, they protect our home, they cuddle with us and make us feel good.

This first sign of a happy dog is sparkling eyes that make eye contact with humans. A happy dog has a healthy interest in food, it has a shiny coat and a frequently wagging tail. A good indication your dog is truly happy is when it rolls on its back with to let you scratch its belly.

Each cat has a personality of its own. Some are attention hogs while others are more aloof. Most cats will become friendly with at least one person in the family, approaching for attention and purring or "talking" to its preferred human. A happy cat has bright eyes and will groom itself. Cats may be a little shy, disappearing when visitors call, but as long as they eat, drink, sleep and poop regularly, your cat is probably okay.

Happy birds will sing while pet rabbits may jump in the air for joy and run around. You can generally tell when a pet is happy by the way it behaves.

The following are some tips on how to keep your pets happy and how to make your home a pet paradise:

- Pets need a place of their own where they feel safe. Dogs may enjoy a pillow, a blanket, or a crate. Cats like kitty condos and out-of-the-way hiding places. Bird have their own cages and a rabbit or ferret will have its own cage. All these various homes require frequent cleaning, for the good health of everybody in the home.

- Pet-proof your home as necessary. Get down on the ground and look around at the same height as your pet. Look for hazards like wires or poisonous plants. Use nonskid rugs on hardwood floors to stop paw pads from sliding; cover wires with foam to prevent chewing.

- Most pets prefer a consistent feeding time. Include healthy food in the recommended amounts for your pet, with healthy snacks to add variety. Do not change the type of food suddenly, but gradually blend a little new food into the old food, increasing the ratio until your pet is eating all new food.

- Your pet should have a consistent supply of water. A pet should never be left outside without water and some form of shelter. Be especially careful about overexposure when the outdoor temperature is at either extreme.

- Most pets need regular exercise every day in order to stay healthy and happy. Walk your dog. Use a laser pointer or a feather on a string to stimulate your cat to play. It is a good idea to exercise with your pet at the same time every day if possible.

- Groom your pet. Brushing out old hair allows you to check for any inconsistency in a pet's coat or skin that may indicate health problems. You will remove any matting before it becomes too extensive, check for evidence of fleas, and make your pet look beautiful at the same time. Cats generally groom themselves and will seldom require a bath, but dogs that play outdoors will require bathing to keep from smelling like dirty dog, or worse.

- When your pet has been very good and done something you can be proud of, make sure to reward it. Lavish praise, treats and toys are great incentives to be good.

- Dogs need socialization so be sure to give your dog opportunity to interact with visitors and other dogs, in addition to the time you spend playing and training.

- Mental stimulation is important for most pets, but especially dogs and cats. Teach them tricks or use toys that hide a treat for them to extract. Small animals may appreciate a maze that holds a treat at the end.

- Cats love to climb and hide. Shelves on the wall for climbing, tunnels, bridges, a scratching post, and cozy hideaways make for a happy kitty. Install a shelf or a padded cat perch in front of a window so your cats can sun themselves and watch wildlife outside.

- Cats also like to stalk and chase almost anything that moves, or pounce.

- Dogs generally love to play catch and hide-and-seek, but they thrive on just being with you.

- Place your dogs in a crate when you are not home. This reduces anxiety and makes them feel safer. It minimizes separation anxiety and prevents them from doing damage to your home.

- Clean a cat's litter box a couple times a day to keep your cat happy and to prevent feline illnesses.

- Pets that go outdoors should be protected by a fence. Ensure that what grows within the fence is not toxic to your pets. Keep adequate water outside for your pets and provide both shade and a safe shelter. Limit your pet's exposure to the elements when the weather reaches either extreme – most dogs and cats are not equipped for either extended heat or cold exposure.

- Pets can experience anxiety when you are away for a period of time. If you go out of town, if you choose not to board your pet, engage a friend to visit once or twice a day to play with your pets and take them outside as necessary.

Before you leave, ensure that the house and the pet's living area is clean. Leave something that smells like you with your pet. An old T-shirt you don't mind getting dirty will work well. Another way to keep pets calm when you are gone is to leave the radio or television playing at a low volume.

Our pets deserve a paradise just like we do. These suggestions will help live happy and comfortable lives as they enhance the character of your home paradise.

Conclusion

I hope this book was able to help you to build your home into the paradise you deserve. The next step is to make a list of your favorite ideas from this book and then start implementing them. You can be the house on the block that your family and neighbors will gravitate towards when they need to be refreshed. Your house can also be a peaceful sanctuary that you get all to yourself sometimes, optimized just the way you like it. Whether you want to entertain others or just have a place of your own that you truly love, let your home be the place that everyone loves.

Remember to nurture your personal inner paradise so that you will have the strength and resources to keep your home a life-giving oasis of healing refreshment that brings joy into your life and others. Set up a plan for developing self-nurturing habits before you do anything else, as you take care of yourself, you will be better equipped to care for the needs of others.

Review the many tips, tricks and strategies for organizing, minimizing, decorating, and maintaining your home and form a plan for implementing your favorite ideas that will help transform your home into a paradise for yourself, your family, your friends, and your acquaintances. This probably won't happen overnight, but make a start today. Little by little, your home will be transformed into a refreshing oasis. Keep on making progress, and in the not too distant future you will be amazed at the improvement in your house, yourself, your mood and your overall life happiness. Take action now to make your own personal paradise here on Earth.

Finally, if you discovered at least one thing that has helped you or that you think would be beneficial to someone else, be sure to take a few seconds to easily post a quick positive review. As an author, your positive feedback is desperately needed. Your highly valuable five star reviews are like a river of golden joy flowing through a sunny forest of mighty trees and beautiful flowers! *To do your good deed in making the world a better place by helping others with your valuable insight, just leave a nice review.*

My Other Books and Audio Books
www.AcesEbooks.com

Health Books

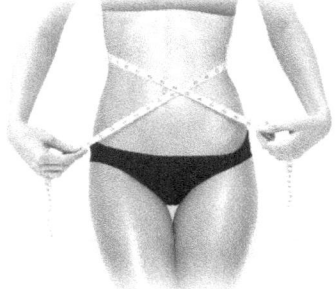

Peak Performance Books

Be sure to check out my audio books as well!

 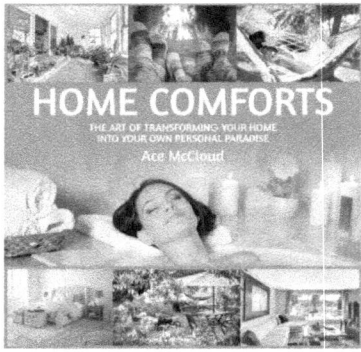 

  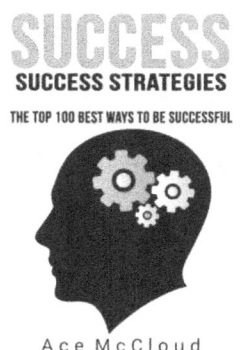

Check out my website at: www.AcesEbooks.com for a complete list of all of my books and high quality audio books. I enjoy bringing you the best knowledge in the world and wish you the best in using this information to make your journey through life better and more enjoyable! **Best of luck to you!**

www.ingramcontent.com/pod-product-compliance
Lightning Source LLC
Chambersburg PA
CBHW051422070526
44584CB00023B/3537